THE ART OF
SURVIVAL

PUBLISHED BY SURVIVAL STATION PUBLICATIONS

WWW.THESURVIVALSTATION.COM

THE ART OF SURVIVAL

Copyright © 2010

SECOND PRINTING 2011

ISBN# 978-1-928737-79-7

Library of Congress Control Number: 2010907389

DEDICATION

To my beautiful and devoted wife of 56years, Libby.

To my supportive and loving family and finally, to the children of the world everywhere and for all time.

—Charles

"Tolerance is the positive and cordial effort to understand another's beliefs, practices and habits without necessarily sharing or accepting them."

—Joshua Liebman

INTRODUCTION: PART ONE

I was young then—only 18—with the bright lights of my life before me; a young man who would finish his education and go on to do wonderful things. You know youth, forever filled with aspirations and enthusiasm for the future. I had no idea what was soon to unfold; the many terrors I was destined to experience; the day-to-day struggle to stay alive with so many odds against me. But...I did survive.

I am old now, at least by most standards. I am indeed an old man, but I remain in good shape (for my age, of course) and my memory still serves me well. And I have done what I believe all "older gentleman" should do: I have become somewhat of a philosopher. Well, as you will soon know, I have seen many things in my life and have experienced many joys and many sorrows. I am fortunate in that I have known love for a woman, a woman who has been my wife for over a half century. I have had a good marriage and a wonderful family! In these ways, I am a very fortunate man. After all, family is more important to me than I have ever declared to those around me, as I am, by and large, a private man. I do not say *I love you* very easily. Perhaps this is a fault of mine, but I believe it is because in the past, I have lost so many whom I've loved. You see, I am among the last of those to recall those hideous times of the Second World War, when I lost many loved ones—friends and family—to the viciousness of the Nazis. I was a prisoner of theirs for six very long years. And yet, I am happy to report that yes, as I said, I survived.

Survival is important, and we are all faced with its challenges. After all, even in peace-time we humans endure psychological, physical and emotional pain along our paths. I think the worst of human suffering is when the pain becomes so harsh that all we want to do is escape ourselves. I have felt this kind of pain, and perhaps you have, too? My first goal in this book, then, is to share "surviving" with you, perhaps to give you greater insights to help you forge ahead even when you feel like the entire world is against you. Oh, don't worry, I do not intend to preach in this book; preaching is not my style. I simply want to share my story with you and if, by chance, you find some value for

I

yourself from my experiences, I will be pleased. Well, I have already admitted that at my age, I have become *somewhat* of a philosopher.

I was born at home in Kielce, Poland, on October 19, 1920, with the help of a midwife, and was raised by my parents, as were my four brothers. All of our lives would be reshaped by the war!

My mother was a lovely and loving woman, a kind and generous woman, while my father was a businessman who was often traditional and sometimes quite stern. I loved them both very much and even today, after such a long time, I can sometimes feel my mother's touch when I reminisce. Both my parents were eventually murdered by the Nazis, as were millions of others. It is perhaps difficult to imagine the horror of it all, the cruelty that so many people endured. I am going to do my best to tell you about it because I want you to be aware that such atrocities can happen again and indeed have from time to time over the decades. After all, I am not alone when it comes to human suffering from the will of the *enslavers of the world,* from people so caught up in their ideologies that they lose their consciences and close down their potential to feel tolerance and understanding for others; such people reject their empathy and take on the nature of evil.

I was raised amongst those who hated Jews merely because we were different. I will soon enough be telling you about that hatred, but for now I just want you to have a little background before I start telling you my story. I want to prepare you for a journey upon which the prospects of survival were extremely slim, a journey where those human commodities like hope and even desire were, so to speak, stripped from our souls. And so, like Kierkegaard characters, *we were left denuded, seeing only the intolerable abyss of ourselves.*

There are moments when a person has become so empty of hope and of life that he prefers to die. I do not mean this in terms of actual death, but rather in terms of a final escape from one's circumstances. Perhaps you have experienced at least a touch of what I am talking about in your own life? Perhaps you have faced financial problems or the loss of a loved one or a lover has abandoned you and you have screamed out, *I wish I were dead.* If you have ever had a moment like this, you will have insight into the feelings that so many people endured day in and day out in the Nazi prison camps and yet... there remained, for most of those same people, the will to survive.

Religious faith, I believe, helps to give such people the courage to carry on in spite of the horrors they are experiencing, in spite of the pain and fear they are enduring. After all, it is strengthening to believe that there is a power much greater than that of your wicked enemies, a power that can lift you over the obstacles and see you through the maze of human suffering that you are confronted with. Indeed, the Torah tells us that every blade of grass has its guardian angel and it is thoughts like this that make survival possible in one's own mind.

This, too, was our little secret as our enemies treated us so inhumanely. We realized that while the evildoers could take away our property and everything else that we held of value in our lives, they could not take away what we kept in our heads or in our hearts.

Surviving the most tragic and devastating circumstances is primarily of the mind and of the heart, since the body can endure the most unimaginable punishments. The very filth that we were forced to live in was the result of unimaginable cruelty, and the hunger we endured was, in so many instances, unimaginable torture in itself. To labor under such conditions was sometimes an unimaginable challenge. And yet, we who survived found ways to keep going, to put one foot in front of the other, as we traveled the unimaginable path that we were on. Do not misunderstand; in such circumstances, luck also played a role. For one thing, we were constantly under armed guards who could murder us at will if they so chose. If someone decided we did not act or look right to them, they could exterminate us upon a whim. We could be chosen to become human "guinea pigs" and sent to some hospital for experimental purposes or have our number called to be gassed or taken before a firing squad. We lived virtually every moment of our imprisonment under these vicious and frightening conditions, never knowing what the next moment would bring. We were *the loathed* and the *dehumanized, the wretched and the unwanted.* We were, beyond all else, the expendable.

III

Surviving under such conditions required, first of all, that we keep our sanity. To overcome the constant humiliation, the stripping of our dignity by those who imagined themselves superior and god-like, condemning Jews and gypsies and so many others to the depths of a living hell, demanded that we keep the faith... in God and in ourselves. It is difficult to imagine, I know, but these kinds of merciless conditions still persist in our world today, only under different names and for different reasons. Indeed, it is much as the anthropologist Marvin Harris reports: "Death squads, secret police, and the torture of prisoners remain at an all-time high, and ethnic, religious and racial groups are killing each other on a grander scale than ever." While he wrote these words in 1989, we humans are still enduring these terrible conditions twenty years later, and it appears they will not stop in the foreseeable future. Man's inhumanity to man has in fact been a continuum since the advent of civilization. This is why I so often feel the urge to create a primal scream that asks; *Why can we not learn from history?*

This book is of course a history book. It is my history! It is the history of a young child being raised with all the hopes and dreams and ambitions of childhood, only to become enslaved by a collection of human beings whose madness murdered nearly six million Jews and aspired to exterminate millions more. Along with Jews, there were hundreds of thousands of Russians, Poles, gypsies, homosexuals and, of course, political prisoners, all sent to *Vernichtungslager* (which means *extermination camps),* where I spent six terrible years learning the *art of survival.*

In regard to all this, I hope you <u>do *not*</u> enjoy my story but rather that you learn from it; I hope that it stirs in you not only the will to survive your most trying times but also to become a link in the chain of events that can bring positive change in our world and to do what you can to make our world a safer, kinder, happier, more secure and loving place. As an older man who has become somewhat of a philosopher, I retain my faith in our potential as a species to create compassion between ourselves, regardless of our differences...I leave this in your hands.

IV

1.

The sociologists tell us that as children, we believe that our parents' world is *the* world, and this was certainly true for me. With only a few exceptions, childhood was a very wonderful place to be. For one thing, we lived in a very nice three-room apartment right next to the city hall, a valuable location where three other Jewish families lived and where fifteen Polish families made their home as well. Things back then were not as they are today; there were no tract houses or lush neighborhoods for successful people to inhabit, and so our apartment was considered a favorable place to live. My parents slept in the bedroom, our maid slept in the kitchen and I slept alongside my four brothers in the living room. No one minded since that was simply how our life was. And, I will add, our lives were much better than many others living in Poland at the time. This was because my father was an industrialist who made shoes and sold them both retail and wholesale. He was a proud, successful man who had done well for himself and his family. In fact, he employed around 100 people—the employees were Polish workers, which I will explain later—and so he kept many families in Kielce earning money and supporting their own families. I, too, would sometimes work for my father doing odd jobs and so forth. After all, I was a boy learning to be responsible.

There are things that mean more to me today than they meant to me back then. I am not talking about my family but rather the "stuff" of our lives, like the old iron cooking stove in the kitchen. The winters in Poland can be brutal, and there is nothing like coming in from the freezing cold and standing in front of a hot fire made of wood and coal. And yes, I confess, much of those olden days are romanticized for me now. Automobiles were rarely seen in Kielce; there was no refrigeration or air conditioning, no telephones and certainly television was not even in our imagination, but we did have a radio. Our drinking water came from the well outside and our bathroom was an outhouse quite a distance from inside the apartment. In the winter, when the snows were deep, the outhouse seemed even farther away than it actually

1

was, but as primitive as it now seems, no one felt inconvenienced because that was our world at the time.

Yes, our world was simple, but even as a child I felt the pains of anti-Semitism. At that age I could not quite grasp why some people hated me because of who I was. Certainly, I knew that religion had a lot to do with it. I believed that I belonged to the chosen people, but no Jewish child or adult ever carried that on his sleeve. Indeed, our religion serves to make us humble, not arrogant; appreciative and not belligerent. In this regard, I think I knew intuitively, even as a child, that some—not all, but some—of the workers held my father in contempt because of his success. He was not only successful but he was also Jewish, and for some, working for a Jew was contemptible. The truth is, however, that my father was a fair man and paid fair wages.

As I say, the fact that Jews were held in contempt just because they were Jews became apparent at a very early age, especially since we children always had to walk to school in groups. We did this because if we walked alone there was always the risk of being beaten up by bigger boys—Polish boys—who, like their parents, despised us.

Because I have been a target of such prejudice both as a child and as an adult, I have thought deeply about anti-Semitism and racism. No one—no one is born hating anyone else; the infant in his or her crib is innocent of such vulgarities as hate and disdain for others. But the infant begins to grow and soon enough his socialization begins. And during those early years of one's socialization, the ideologies, dogmas, superstitions and biases of the significant others in a child's life are passed down as legacies of the mind. Hitler, for a prime example, understood the techniques of socially engineering the youth and used them to his advantage... but I will be talking about that diabolic demagogue a little later. My point here is simply that every child is indoctrinated with the concepts of his parents and teachers and other adults in his life, and those concepts influence how the child grows up to view the world of others. As I have always said, *if one deems the rose bush a thorn bush, then that is what it becomes.* A little food for thought, is it not?

2

Anyway, when I was a young boy I was bored a lot of the time in Kielce. There was just so little to do, especially in the winters. There was only one movie house in town and one theater hall, and while none of us boys were given a weekly allowance, our parents treated us often with ice cream and a movie. There was much more to do in the summer: we had a baseball field and a park that we liked going to. We loved to bicycle, too! I actually liked going to school—at least, most of the time—because my friends were there and from the time I was around eight years old and just starting school, we would meet and walk together, always talking and laughing but also always on the lookout for bigger boys who might attack us. Sometimes the winter temperature would be ten or twenty below, but we were used to that and anyway, we had warm coats to wear. In thinking back, I don't recall any of us having any serious illness. There was a Jewish hospital in town and while doctors made house calls for a very small fee, we were treated at home. That is, when I or my brothers took sick with a bad cold or something, it was my mother's loving hands that healed us.

Sometimes, when I think back to those times, I'm astonished by the changes I have witnessed over the years. In Kielce, back then, the fire department had but one fire engine and that engine was pulled by four horses. I can see it vividly in my mind, even to this day. It was, as people say, a different world then, a world that most Americans call *the good old days*. Well, as I say, they were simpler times, a world without pop-up toasters or many other conveniences. Today's children feel neglected if they don't have their own computer, and that strikes me as being a signal of where technology will be taking us over the rest of this century. I only hope that the children growing up now will bring peace and love into the world, that they will heed the lessons of our human history and use all the wonderful things they have wisely.

In any case, when I talk about anti-Semitism I do not want to give the impression that every Polish person hated the Jews. We had very good friends who were mostly Catholic and who were as kind and friendly as can be. On the other hand, we were a private people, really. We had our own schools and of course, our own religion, our own traditions and customs. We were raised to mind our own business and, as the saying goes, *to live and let live*. I am glad to report that we knew many Polish people who believed this way also.

What we were unaware of, however, were the changes occurring in Germany. We had no idea at the time that our lives were destined to be changed, nor did we have the slightest notion that the quiet streets of Kielce were destined to become a war zone. In fact, at the time, if we even heard the name of Adolf Hitler, it was in passing and we thought little about it. The rumors of what was really going on would not begin for at least a few more years and so, for sure, no one suspected the horrors that awaited us.

It is at this juncture that I want to return to the subject of *indoctrination*. While the children of Kielce (as in nearly all other places) studied geography, reading, writing and so forth, the children of Germany were being taught that they belonged to the superior race and that Jews were sub-human... along with a few others that Hitler deemed unworthy of life itself. Indeed, while we boys were singing our songs and playing our games, the boys in Germany were entering the Jungvolk at age ten. Yes, Hitler was pre-planning his Nazi Army by indoctrinating the children of his land with gross ideals and ideologies. Each ten year old boy took the following oath:

> *In the presence of this blood banner which represents our Fuehrer, I swear all my energies and my strength to the Savior of our Country, Adolf Hitler. I am willing and ready to give up my life for him, so help me God. One People, one Reich, one Fuehrer.*

Imagine the corruption of the young minds who were brainwashed this way; they were to become Hitler's thugs and murderers in the guise of soldiers. But Hitler had a plan and that plan had been written while he, himself, was in prison; the book was titled *Mein Kampf* (My Struggle), but it was mostly a sharing of his political ambitions and philosophy. In fact, he stated in the narrative most of what he intended to do. He was wise enough not to be in a hurry, however, and knew it was more important for the German people to believe that their Aryan race was superior to all others and that, yes, they were destined to rule the world. Remember, no ruler, dictator,

4

tyrant or president declares war without first indoctrinating the general citizenry to support it. By the time Adolf Hitler was ready to make his move, in 1939, he had the vast majority of his country socially engineered to support his every whim. After all, the fatherland was going to master the world, was it not? The fatherland was going to cleanse the world of Jews and other undesirables, was it not? The fatherland was going to produce the master race, was it not? And in spite of the fact that all this sounds like some notion of a comic book villain, this is what Hitler preached and this is what the majority of Germans advocated in the real world, what so many were willing to kill and die for. But as difficult as it is to believe, Hitler built his short-lived empire on a platform of racism and nationalism, a platform that would lead to millions of deaths and untold suffering. Nevertheless, during the mid-1930s in Kielce, no one suspected what was on the far horizon. To us, life was just going on as usual.

It seems, however, that as the later years of the 1930s unfolded, there was a little more prejudice growing. I am not sure if this is true, but I know walking to school we began taking more slurs from boys and hearing more warnings of what they might do to us. Lucky for me, however, I had my older brother Szymon to protect me, as he had no fear of fighting and could handle himself admirably. By this time I was in High School. High School was a good mile away from our home, and a lot can happen in a mile when you are the target of hatefulness, so it was good to have a big brother who knew how to fight.

There was something else: One of the joys we had in Kielce was to go to the park and walk amongst the trees or just sit by the banks of the lake. One warm summer day, however, we decided to go to the park to play and to relax... but there was a sign at the entrance that read, "*No dogs or Jews allowed.*" Yes, anti-Semitism was escalating, we had no idea why.

2.

By 1937-38 the rumors were pouring in about what was happening to the Jews in Germany and how Hitler had built a most powerful army. There were pogroms in some parts of Poland, that is, places resembling German and Russian concentration camps, where many Jews were sent without a trial or even being given a hearing of any kind! There were no pogroms in our area, but we knew of them and we felt the tension growing between the Poles and ourselves. One day, my brother Seweryn had gone to the park, disregarding the signs that had been posted there, and was badly beaten by two Polish boys who attacked him. But by then it was clear that the anti-Semitism was getting worse in town, so it was fortunate that we had our own Jewish centers, with the McCabe Club having its own tennis courts, volleyball, ice skating rink and basketball court. We were, of course, grateful for this, especially since us teenagers had a lot of energy to expend. Most importantly, however, our home life was happy and had always felt secure. My mother was a bright, pleasant person, kind and loving. My father was devoted to his religious practices and so he was more stoic-minded in his way but, as I say, we were happy at home. Content!

We had relatives in town and so we would visit them from time to time. During those visits the adults would talk about what they had heard about Germany, and the fears grew of Germany's vast military machine being put into action. At home my mother would sometimes voice her opinion, saying that we should probably leave and go someplace where it would be safe. My father, however, would not hear of it. I can still hear his voice, *"Oy Vey, everything will be all right. Don't worry so much!"* I wish now that he had worried because had we left when my mother intuitively felt that we should, we would have been just fine. I understand, though; I realize that my father had a business established and we were settled as a family. In these ways the future looked bright for us, and so it would have been difficult to just pack up and move away, to leave so much behind. Still, that is what we should have done. *Ah, the value of hindsight, eh?*

For at least two years, however, and essentially unbeknownst to the Polish people, the Polish leadership and military had been preparing for an invasion by Germany, and so the writing was on the wall so to speak: *trouble was brewing.* We had even heard rumors of this, and this alone should have been enough to uproot us and send us to safety, but we were not alone... thousands of Jews in Kielce hung on to the hope that nothing terrible was going to happen, that somehow those winds of war would blow over and all would remain as it had always been.

Before going on with my story, I wish to clear something up that has been said about us Jews concerning those war years. That is, that we did not resist our enemies and passively marched to the concentration camps (so to speak) like cattle on the way to the slaughter house. This is not true. It is, however, important to understand that we are, in general, a people of deep traditions and religious devotions, of family life and service to our communities. Kielce was no exception, although in that city—my hometown—we did not live under the Torah tradition and were instead more influenced by the Polish culture. We were, at the same time, determined to build the city into an everlasting place, a place where we as individuals and as a people would live in peace and harmony and where our children and our children's children would inherit what we had socially constructed. This, it can be said, is the center of the Jewish heart, something to be achieved through arduous work and yes, through faith! As a result we were not an armed people back then, nor were we a belligerent people. We were, in general, only interested in creating a solid foundation that would be eternal. One does not have to be Jewish to understand this drive. That is, to simply live in peace, in freedom and in at least some relative prosperity. As a result we were, in general, an industrial people and, truth be told, we were a successful people. The Kielce industries were eventually dominated by Jewish manufacturers, shop owners and so forth. The Zaganski family owned and operated the lime kilns that supplied lime to all of Poland; they were indeed very rich! In fact, before the war the Polish government had forced us to replace Jewish workers with Polish workers, a reason my father's employees were all but exclusively Polish. Nevertheless, this success story of our people had

7

also occurred in Germany and especially because of the Great Depression, jealousies and resentments against the Jews had escalated. The general populations were poor and in the end, impoverished and hungry. This is a major reason why Hitler's promise of world domination and superiority worked so well, why it was so easy to create the Jew as the enemy. As I have said, in general all the Jew wanted was to mind his own business. He was simply not prepared for the kind of armed and brutal aggression that awaited him; he was naïve in believing that somehow all would be well.

I was eighteen years old when the war started, but before the war I was like most others: I lived in the hope that conditions in Poland would improve and that at long last we Jews would be treated like normal citizens. All I wanted was to finish my education and have my chance at building a happy life. This was true of my brothers, as well. In fact, my brother Moniek had recently become engaged and he was filled with happy dreams of his own. But then all those frightening rumors manifested into stark realities. The invasion of Poland, also called the September Campaign, began. World War II had been started by the invasion of Poland by Nazi Germany, the Soviet Union and a small contingency of Slovak soldiers.

The Polish military did their best to defend their homeland, but they had few weapons and no one wins wars by charging tanks on horseback. The final battle occurred on October 6th and the German and Russian forces were suddenly in control of all of Poland.

We stayed inside the entire day that the Nazi troops marched through town with their Polish prisoners, men who looked as beaten as they were; men who looked too frail and too worn to go much further! The sight was too unbearable for my mother and so she dared to run out and give the prisoners bread, water and apples. She risked her life that day, but thankfully she managed to return to the apartment house without incident. None of us knew what was going to happen, but after a time my brother Seweryn showed that he was the smart one. He and some of his friends left Kielce, heading toward the Russian border. Captured, he was sent deep into Russia where he was made a slave laborer, and he remained there (and so remained alive) throughout the entire war years. Unlike the Germans, the Russians did not murder those that they enslaved. As for the rest of us remaining in Kielce, we quickly became targets. Soon enough the Polish children wanting to win the favor of the Nazi soldiers were pointing out places where Jews lived, and almost immediately Nazis were banging on the doors of all Jewish residences.

After the *knock* came at our door, I was told to follow them outside. Regarding this, I want you to know that I was not like a sheep willing to simply follow the shepherd to the sacrificial altar but I could not fight nor run nor hide. Remember, I was confronting a conquering army who had quickly taken over everything, including all the government buildings in town, and yes, I was scared! I did not know if I would be walking out to face a firing squad or not, but I knew for sure if I disobeyed I would be killed then and there. I wanted to survive!

This was the real power of the Nazis. They were willing killers and everyone knew this. Indeed, as soon as they marched into Kielce, they began confiscating everything from furs to jewelry, paintings, silver and everything else of value; they even took the gold from the teeth of those they killed. And if anyone argued with them, they lost their lives. It was very clear—*they were the masters and we were their slaves.* And so when I walked out of the apartment, I simply had no choice. If I had refused I would not only have gotten myself shot but maybe my entire family, as well, and I knew this all too well.

On the street I was confronted by a young Nazi who looked to be no older than sixteen; he was armed and held a rifle on me. I did not know it then, but today I am convinced that the young trooper was one of Hitler's youths, a boy who had been indoctrinated to hate Jews since he was ten years old; a kid who believed in one race and one Fuehrer and would easily shoot me without hesitation. After all, he had become the persona of his neat, brown uniform with the swastikas that so boldly symbolized his superiority and arrogance.

He marched me through the city streets now cluttered with broken glass and other debris from the grenade attacks and other fear tactics of the takeover. By then the streets of Kielce were quiet, a deadly silence, really. Ghostly in a way! I still did not know if I was headed to my own death or not, and so my mind was swarming with thoughts in one moment and then empty of any thinking at all in the next. Under such stress the brain becomes hyperactive, really, but it is difficult to explain. I can only say that I kept walking and that I was very nervous.

We walked for around a mile and finally I was directed to turn into a building that was occupied by men in black uniforms also adorned with swastikas; the uniforms themselves were threatening, but of course, Hitler was a very detailed tyrant who was very aware of the dramatic. In any case, I was ordered to clean up the building, as they wanted to make their office there. The building was in shambles, with glass and other debris covering the floor. My eyes met with six other prisoners who had been ordered there to be part of the cleanup crew, too. I could see the fear and apprehension in their eyes, on the very expressions that shadowed their faces, and I wondered if I looked as gaunt.

We worked hard, picking everything up by hand, and loaded it into a large dump truck. I had worked hard and steady that day and had been obedient but that didn't matter; a couple of the Nazis just began beating me with their batons and making slurs about me being a Jew. I could not fight back and was helpless, so I had no option other than to take the beating and hope they would stop. This was in October, and the Kielce air had already turned a little icy, but as soon as the beating was over the same soldiers threw cold water on me. I was beaten like that more than once that day, and I am convinced that it was just cruel sport for those soldiers.

After the truck was loaded we were ordered to climb on, which we did. We would have to unload the trash! The ride was not very long, just to the outskirts of town to a spot where other debris had been dumped. We were ordered to start unloading, and as we unloaded the trash from the truck the Nazi soldiers began target practice, making sure the bullets came close to us. It was very nerve-racking to work under those conditions, but this was their way of telling us that we were mere puppets on their string and that they could cut the string anytime that they chose. We didn't need such a reminder.

It had turned dark by the time we returned to town and as I sat in the big bed of the empty dump truck with the other prisoners, I worried what was to happen next. I felt exhausted and hungry, although I do not think I could have eaten anything. My stomach was so upset from the experiences and my back was aching from the beatings. Finally the truck stopped and we were back at the building where we were told to *climb down from the truck*. After this, however, the first relief of our horrible day of uncertainty arrived: We were released to go home.

Unless a person has experienced being fully subordinated, as I had been that day, has been at the mercy of cruel others who have the power of life and death over you, it may be difficult to identify with the freedom one feels by simply being able to *go home*. I think I knew then that I was going to survive—or maybe it was merely surviving that day that gave me such high hopes. I don't know, but just being able to go home, I felt a little like the butterfly must feel when it leaves it chrysalis—a rebirth of sorts, a flight into liberation.

Many things happened over the next few weeks and months. It had not been difficult at all for the Nazis to round up all the Jews. It was not only the Poles pointing out where we lived. In Poland there was a rule called Police Registration. This meant that every citizen had to be registered in City Hall, giving information that included race, age and religion. The Nazis had access to these files. Actually, when the war came to Kielce and many apartment buildings were being destroyed, my father finally agreed to pack up and leave. We planned on going to the city of Lwow in the Eastern part of Poland but it was impossible to find transportation and so we ended up moving in with our Uncle David; he had a house not far from our apartment. There was no escaping and so at that juncture we were trapped.

What might come as a surprise is that my father had reopened his shoe store only two days after the occupation. Was life going to return to normal? We had moments of believing that it might. That was wishful thinking, of course. There had been a P.O.W. camp built near the city where many Polish soldiers and officers were sent, along with select Jews and others. We were all in constant danger of being sent there... or someplace worse.

The following days did not pass without incident. For one thing, it seemed that the Nazis constantly made up new rules for us to abide by and as a demonstration of their unlimited power, they arrested people and executed several. The Nazis had also taken over all the best places—hotels, office buildings and so forth—while the regular German Army took over all the Polish military buildings and barracks. Their presence was everywhere; a dark cloud that persisted over us and kept us in the deepest shadows of depression. We prayed often; we had no other hope, no other place to turn.

I do not recall how many days had passed, perhaps a week or more, but in an unexpected moment a group of Gestapo men entered my father's place of business, took his keys and closed the store. Afterwards they searched our house and took our camera and a few other things of value before leaving. Then we were ordered to work at the store without compensation, which we did, but a few months later, they moved my father's business to a new location and stopped manufacturing shoes. They only kept the retail store open! At that time, the Nazis had put a Polish man in charge of the store, and so my father then had nothing more to do with the business. As a result, the hope that all might return to normal was suddenly gone forever.

3.

It is nearly impossible to explain the thoughts and feelings we endured when our entire world was suddenly transformed and tyrannized by enemy soldiers, soldiers that loathed everything about us, including our religion. While it is true that we Jews in Poland had always experienced the pangs of anti-Semitism, the prejudice held against us by the Nazis was sadistic. They often murdered, robbed and tortured our people for the sport of it. How could they do this, you might ask, how could any human being be this cruel to other human beings? To understand this, you must realize that through their training and indoctrinations, Jews were seen as subhuman and so we had been dehumanized and made into "things." There is also something else. There is an old saying that tells us that *power corrupts and absolute power corrupts absolutely.* The Nazis and other German authority had "absolute" power over us!

In any case, there was no time for adjusting to our new circumstances. It was as if in one instant all was normal and in the next nothing was normal; the life we had always known in Kielce was gone and a hellish reality had formed in its place. It was surreal, like being trapped in a lucid dream from which there is no awakening. I cannot explain it more than this except, perhaps, to say that the actuality of it all twisted in the pits of our stomachs as we continued on from one moment to the next. There was nothing else that we could do.

After a few months our routines were disrupted again. My brothers Szymon and Abe and myself were rounded up with around 600 other young men—boys, really—and marched to the Synagogue. We were ordered inside where we were kept prisoners for three days. We were under the command of an S.S. Captain who took pleasure in our suffering. His name was Geier. I have never forgotten it, and I remember him just as clearly: a man who wore his arrogance and cruelty in the very strut of his walk, in the very gloating that reflected in his eyes. We were his toys, his source of pleasure. With a single pointing of a finger he could have us beaten or killed and so we tried not to look at him, not to do anything to draw attention to ourselves. This was our only defense.

We spent three devastating days and night inside the Synagogue. I say "devastating" because there was no running water and no bathrooms, so our place of religious service and prayer was necessarily desecrated. None of us captives were insensitive to this, but nothing could be done about it. We were not permitted to talk with each other, so few of our thoughts were shared except on the expressions of our faces. Over the two nights that we were detained we slept on the floor and were given little to eat. And, as always, we wondered if we were waiting for our deaths so the minutes passed like hours. An important part of surviving is to control your anxiety, however. Anxiousness can cause you to make mistakes!

Finally we found out that we were being sent to Lublin. In fact, it was Hauptman Geier who gave us the news. He had strutted in with his shepherd dog and bodyguards to declare our orders. We assembled and made our way outside. There had been many guards that stood watch over us in the Synagogue and we were greeted with even more outside. They were S.S. troops with German and Polish police! Soon enough, they marched us to the train station while a crowd of Poles gathered to watch the precession, a parade of the doomed, they probably imagined, as some were yelling their cruelties at us. Perhaps some thought that they were pleasing the Nazis, but others were simply venting their hatefulness. There were also those who only watched, those who seemed to feel sadness for us. They remained silent, of course. After all, to show a Jew kindness was to endanger oneself. As for us young men, we were obliged to simply follow "the herd."

At the train station we were loaded into boxcars, around 80 people to each car. Once loaded the doors were shut, as were the small windows, and so quite quickly it became nearly impossible to breathe and the heat became nearly unbearable. All this occurred at the end of June, and so being stuffed in those boxcars was like being in an inferno. Admittedly, I do not recall what I was thinking as the train pushed forward, but I am sure I wondered about my parents and the rest of my

14

family and prayed for their safety and for my own. I might have thought about my brother Moniek, who had attended college in Warsaw. We had lots of family in Warsaw, so I would have thought about them, as well.

Moniek had met a young lady in Warsaw who he had written to us about, and they were engaged. They had decided to move on to Lithuania, where her family lived, and to be married there. The major reason for this decision was that the college where Moniek was attending   passed a rule that demanded all Jewish students to sit on the left side of the classroom. Even though the rule had been a government order, Moniek had rebelled against it and had taken many beatings for his rebellion. And it was because of this that he would have been—or was—marked as a *troublemaker.* Trouble-making Jews were soon eliminated, and so Lithuania sounded very enticing to them.

As I say, I don't really recall what thoughts occupied my mind as the journey in those horrible conditions of the cattle cars continued, but I struggled to remain hopeful and...brave. Fear, after all, can be an overwhelming tyrant that, in a term, weakens the spirit and can eventuate into an impossible obstacle to cross. Fear, after all, does not need ropes or chains to tie you down since it can restrain you by its very nature and deem you a prisoner of yourself. I witnessed many people over the years of my captivity whose fear alone became their worst enemies. And of course the Nazis wanted to be feared, as this was part of their psychological ploy to control!

None of this means that I was not scared. I was often scared, but who would not be under such conditions? On the other hand, real fear is not the same as being really scared. Being scared makes you cautious but, like a river, you keep moving around all the obstacles until you reach your destination. Using this same metaphor, fear is like a dam—the dam stops the river from even trying (or attempting) to get where it wants to be. Do you see what I'm saying?

While it seemed somewhat of a lifetime, we only traveled a day and a night to reach the town of Lublin. Nevertheless, when the doors of the boxcar opened, I do not think that I will ever forget the preciousness of the cool breeze blowing against my skin. Indeed, those moments of relief were seen on all the faces of the prisoners who had been cooped together in the terrible heat, and I suspect that none of us who survived will ever forget the value of fresh air. I know that I will not!

We were made to line up as soon as we were off the train. A few local people had already gathered to appease their curiosities or to find some kind of pleasure in watching enslaved human beings being dominated by their masters. And the S.S. soldiers who had been waiting for us made quite a show of their power as they barked out their orders telling us exactly what to do, and pity the poor person who did not or could not obey.

I am sure that I did not realize it then but all the Nazis were *"method"* actors in many ways. They became their costumes, their swastikas and shiny boots; they believed that they were the "master race," after all, and so they mirrored themselves as masters permitting one to live and another to die. And so it was that day we arrived in Lublin.

Only a few minutes after we had been formed into lines, the march through the town began. We prisoners were no threat and were doing what we were told and yet, this was not enough to satisfy their arrogance. The Nazis began beating us randomly with horsewhips, making us run through the streets. When one is struck with such whips the skin is invariably cut and the pain is harsh, sometimes excruciating. But we dared not stop. We must have run for at least four or five miles under those conditions, until we reached the S.S. barracks. Once inside, my brother Szymon carefully removed his shirt, a painful experience that exposed his bloody back, which had already turned black and blue. There was nothing to treat his wounds with.

We spent three days in those barracks under heavy guard but basically left to ourselves in that terrible chamber of the mind that wonders what will happen next. Well, the next morning some S.S. troops entered and took away 60 boys to be sent to Belzec. We thought then that Belzec was a labor camp but we would learn years later that it

16

was among the first extermination camps that were being constructed, even at that early juncture of the war.

While talking about Belzec, I will digress for a moment from my story to tell you about the concentration (death) camps where so many of us were in constant jeopardy of being sent. The Belzec camp is representative of most: Actually the Belzec facility began as a labor camp but was restructured for mass exterminations. Compared to future extermination centers, however, Belzec was small. It was divided into two sections, both of which were surrounded with barbed wire. There were watchtowers around the perimeter to keep order and to keep anyone from attempting to escape. There were train tracks leading into the camp so prisoners could be transported inside the compound and unloaded from boxcars. Belzec was commanded by around 30 S.S. men and a guard company of Ukrainians. There were also "laboring" Jews who were forced to carry out duties that were associated with the murdering process. These Jewish people had been selected from other labor camps and from the Jewish community itself.

Most typically when prisoners arrived they were both mentally and physically exhausted from the terrible conditions of the trip and from other past experiences under Nazi rule, so they were easy to control. As soon as they were off the train the prisoners were separated into three groups—men, women and children. They were thereafter marched to barracks where they were forced to undress. Their clothing and other personal items were collected by the laborers and taken to warehouses.

The prisoners were kept unaware of their fate and told that they had arrived in a transit camp where they needed to shower and clean up, so the undressing did not seem threatening to them. The women's heads were also shaved. As soon as the shaving process was over, they were brutally shoved into gas chambers made to look like showers, as were the men and children after their preparations. Actually the death houses were in the second section of the camp. There the three gas chambers had been built in a wooden barrack. The barrack was constructed with a double wall with sand in between the

17

walls; there were two airtight doors, one for the prisoners to enter and an exit door to have their corpses removed. (The 60 boys separated from us at Lublin were among the first to be exterminated at this camp).

There was a large diesel engine just outside the barrack that piped in carbon monoxide. When gas began pouring in, instead of shower water, the prisoners realized that they were going to die and the process was agonizing, since it took up to thirty minutes to complete. The entire process from arrival at the camp took around three hours. In those early days it is said that around 600,000 thousand Jews and an unknown count of Gypsies were murdered like this. These early models of death facilities were soon to be enlarged and improved in that the wooden barracks would be built of brick and the bodies could be disposed of in ovens as opposed to open, pit fires.

As a point of interest, the Belzec camp was closed in 1943 but guards had to be posted to keep the local people from excavating the grounds seeking valuables. During this time the Nazis decided to plough over the entire compound and turn the grounds into a farm. A Ukrainian guard was chosen to be the farmer.

After our three day stay in the Barrack at Lublin we were marched back to the train tracks and packed back into boxcars for transportation—another miserable, mind-numbing experience of thick, hot air and cramped conditions. Little did we know then how lucky we were not to be going to Belzec! We arrived in Hrubieszow around noon on a Saturday.

I will never forget the town of Hrubieszow. After disembarking the train we were loaded on the back of trucks for transport. And as in other places the local residence lined the streets to see the procession of slaves being taken to their destinations. We were not bothered by this, as by then we were used to being stared at like animals in a zoo. But the Jews living in Hrubieszow were daring. They did not strive to please their German captors at all. Instead they showered us with apples, pears, bread and *challah*. (Challah is also a kind of bread). This was an unexpected experience and one that refreshed and gladdened our hearts. Indeed, this brave showing of kindness and generosity strengthened our spirits as the food strengthened our bodies. Our world had suddenly been made a little better.

When I think back to that day I am always reminded of the words of Anne Frank who, while in hiding, wrote in her diary, *"How wonderful it is that nobody needs to wait a single moment before starting to improve the world."* As an old man who has turned into somewhat of a philosopher I am always stirred by this young girl's observation and I am reminded of Gandhi's wisdom as well. Gandhi, after all, told us that *each of us must become the change that we desire for the world.* If only these wisdoms alone were put into human action, all the unnecessary suffering would simply go away.

In any case, the trucks continued through town and on to Mircze, Poland, nearer the Russian border, where my brothers and I ended up in a prison camp. We wondered what would be happening to us there.

4.

We began our stay at Mircze in a dilapidated building with dirt floors, but soon enough we moved from there and into a large barn in a nearby field. The barn was quite old, too, and had turned gray from being weatherworn. Indeed, under different circumstances and in other times a passerby would probably have found the entire scene quaint and pastorally charming, but for us prisoners there was nothing nice or esthetic about it. To us that old barn was merely an extension of the miserable and filthy conditions that we had been continually forced to live in. And it was!

There were still a few cows and pigs kept in the barn but obviously once upon a time this old, gray relic from the past had housed a wealth of livestock. Indeed, mixed with the smell of the animals that were kept there in the present, there was that thick stench of dung and dirt ground together over past decades that is common to all old and neglected barns.

My brothers Abe and Szymon, along with myself and other prisoners, found places to sleep and did our best to make our beds a little softer by piling straw on top of the ground. After all, the dirt floor of the barn, after so many years of being trampled and walked on, was hard as cement. But, as I say, it was quite old, built a half century before or longer ago than this—we did not know. What we did know is that we were stuck there and so we had to make the best of it.

The barn doors were never locked, day or night, but there was no hope for escape. Ukrainian guards and guard dogs were kept on 24 hour watch. The Ukrainians, in their black, menacing uniforms, were armed, so any hope of running away was merely wishful thinking. The chances of actually escaping were, as the saying goes, slim to none.

We had been sent to Mircze to work on a road. This was extremely hard labor and while we didn't know it at the time, we were "paving the way" for the Germans to attack Russia. Having roads in good shape was part of their strategy! At the same time, we were hoping that the Russian Army would come in and put a stop to our suffering. In that remote place we did not know about Pearl Harbor or the Americans entering the war so Russia remained our hope as becoming the power that would defeat the Germans. Living under Russian rule did not promise the freedom we desired, but at least the Russians were not as cruel or murderous as the Nazis were; at least under the Russians, we would be able to restructure and rebuild our lives. As it was we were treated as slaves, dehumanized and made into *beasts of burden.*

The Nazis at Mircze seemed even more arrogant than in other places we had been, more dictatorial and yes, more authoritative—pompous, if you will—which made them all the more dangerous. Looking back on the situation, I realize that the German armies had had many successes in their aggressions by then and so they were *feeling* as unconquerable as Hitler's propaganda had been telling them that they were, experiencing the egocentricity of believing that they were indeed the master race come to rule the world. At the same time, there was a reverse of this mental state. That is, some prisoners were becoming the slaves that they were treated as being. They were simply doing what they were told mechanically and so, in their way, they had lost the spirit of being a self while taking on the nature of the oppressed.

I will tell you at this juncture that this defeats the desire to survive and to overcome, much less to succeed. When life becomes extremely difficult, as it does for many people along their paths, it is essential to never confuse yourself with your situation. That is, you are not your poverty or your debt, the rags you are wearing or the old "Junker" car that you drive. Do you follow me? I hope so, because many people become devastated by their troubles and begin mirroring themselves as the devastation itself. Once this happens, human will is compromised and only more defeat and failure follows.

During those long and tragic war years we had everything—everything—taken from us: Our homes, our education, our money, our keepsakes and, in countless instances, those whom we loved! In the process, we were made prisoners of a cruel and heartless regime and

21

treated like chattel, beaten and often starved, while always confronting the possibility of being murdered. The courage then was not letting loose of the self and so not becoming the slave while in slavery: In other words, to maintain a sense of meaning and purpose inside ourselves and *to simply keep the faith* that we would eventually overcome the terrible circumstances of our lives. In this same regard, I have had many people ask me how, after more than half a century, my wife and I continued to be such strong and loving companions. I always tell them that we learned many, many years ago to fight our problems instead of each other. Do you see what I am saying here? *We never identified ourselves with the best and worse conditions of our lives.* There were those in the prison camps who became incapable of doing this, of separating themselves from their challenges and as a result, not many of them survived; they had become the devastation that they were going through and thus became the slaves they had been told that they were by the Nazis. I mention all this because I believe it is worth thinking about...after all, the necessity to survival is to survive, and surviving means never giving up and so never confusing yourself with your situation. That is, as I say, to be a slave without ever taking on the nature of a slave!

In any case, life was hard in Mircze, especially when the weather turned cold. We were worked 10 to 12 hours a day, and when the ground was frozen the work became all the more challenging; some days it was difficult to just keep going. On the other hand, the only reason that we were being kept alive was because we were workers. In those days there was little automation and so manual labor was a great commodity for the German initiative. After all, back then, it was the pick and shovel that moved mountains!

Life was not all bad. There was a house not far from the barn and a Mrs. Kowalska lived there with her two daughters. We befriended her and we could see in her eyes that she had much empathy for us. As a result, she would sometimes bring us food that she prepared in her kitchen. The homemade cooking was a treat for us, and it made her happy to see us gobble it up. It is not so strange that such acts of kindness were engraved in our hearts and to this very day, I remember her well and can sometimes still see her gentle smile.

My brother Szymon got somewhat of a break after we had been in camp a few weeks. He was chosen to work in the Post Office. This left Abe and me continuing to labor on the road repairs. Then, not too long after Szymon had left, a delegation was sent from our hometown to distribute clothing, soap, blankets and food. Abe and I were elected to do the distributing, which we did. There was something else. Those in the delegation had a private conversation with my brother and me, telling us that they wanted to bribe those in charge to release around 85 men who had families to support. They wanted to know if we thought that a bribe would work. Abe and I said that we could arrange a meeting with the Ukrainian commandants, which we did. Because they wanted money to buy vodka and to fatten their purses they readily contrived to release the prisoners who had wives and children. They did this by filling out paperwork that said those specific prisoners were ill, and the ploy worked! Abe and I became heroic at home because we had been so intrinsic in making the arrangement, and that pleased us. We were also pleased to have helped anyone escape that hellhole in Mircze.

The nights by then were freezing cold and the barn had no heat. To make things worse, there were a lot of rats running about. In fact, I was bitten by one but thankfully the wound was not very deep. I still gave some thought to possible infection, though. After all, getting sick and being unable to work got many people shot, so keeping on one's feet was vital to our survival. In all the camps but very much so in Mircze, if a guard saw you slow down or if you weren't working in a way that he thought you should, there could be grave consequences. Abe and I knew this and we were concerned, because neither of us was feeling very good at the time. A winter "bug," we thought, or maybe it was just because we weren't getting enough to eat? We didn't know.

It didn't matter. Somehow Szymon's wife, Luba, had managed to bribe someone and get us released from Mircze. After our release we were taken home in a horse drawn wagon. The ride was long, uncomfortable and very cold, but we didn't mind. We were breathing free air for a change, and being away from the back-breaking work was relief in itself. When we finally arrived in Kielce, our hearts were already pumping with anxiousness to see our parents and when we did, the reunion was filled with emotion. After all, none of us knew if we were ever to see each other again and so if ever the wise, old advice that tells a person to *expect the worst but hope for the best* was applicable, it was during those days. After all, we were all pawns on the Nazis' chessboard and so our lives were in their hands.

It is difficult to explain but just being in a room with my parents again and being able to feel my mother's touch and hear her voice was a precious gift. Even under the circumstances, there was deep warmth in the room, a deep joy. We were all illuminated with love and caring for one another. At least we had those moments and those moments would belong to us...forever.

The joy was not to last, however. Abe and I continued to feel worse. Our temperatures rose and our bodies began aching. We were sick! Our parents were able to get us to the hospital where a few Jewish nurses remained. Our illness was recognized immediately. We had Typhoid Fever. There were others in the hospital with the same disease.

Typhoid comes from contaminated water and/or food. That is, when sewage is not thoroughly separated from what is eaten or drunk, the contamination develops. Because Typhoid is a fecal contamination and we had been living in such filth in the barn, it is no wonder that we came down with it. And coming down with it in those days was all but a death sentence. Jews in the hospital were not allowed to be given antibiotics and so there was not much that could be done for us. Those treating us, however, did what they could and after around five weeks, both Abe and I were able to leave the hospital. We regained our strength at home.

We had been lucky again, since at many hospitals run by the Nazis, sick Jews were simply injected with gasoline to get rid of them. In any case, we were "at home" again, but home was not at all like it once was.

All the Jews had been ordered out of their own homes, given only fifteen minutes to pack up what they could. Afterwards we were marched to the ghetto in town, a slum area where the poorest of the poor lived. They had evacuated the Poles and replaced them with us. There were around 20,000 of us packed in an area of only a few blocks and mostly stuffed into small apartments with two, three and four families sharing the rooms. We made do; there were no alternatives.

Primarily, the ghetto had been turned into a prison compound. The entire section of town was surrounded by a fence and guarded by Polish police and armed Ukrainian guards on the outside. Jewish police worked the inside, but I will explain this a little later. There were spies everywhere in order to keep the Nazis informed of any plans to rebel or even of anyone speaking insubordinate words against the Germans. The spies even reported what was going on in the "private" lives of the Jews, although there was little privacy for any of us. Not all the spies were Poles or ethnic Germans. There were a few Jews that spied for the Nazis, too. Jews that thought they were buying their safety by being informers. I personally do not know how they lived with themselves but it is not for me to judge. And anyway, in the end, they were all shot because the Nazis did not like Jews knowing too much of their business. However, what still amazes me from time to time is that all the Jews that informed were merely used and then murdered and yet, it seems others would quickly take their places. Thankfully, there were only a handful of Jewish spies among us, but that handful caused a lot of people a lot of grief.

In thinking of the above, I am nearly always reminded of that old saying that tells us, *adversity introduces a man to himself.* There is a strong truth in this, I believe.

Around the time that Abe and I were fully recovered from our illness the Jewish council ordered us to go to work at Kadzielnia, the stone quarry. The Polish police who patrolled inside the fences of the Ghetto also took their orders from them, although the Nazis had appointed a new Chief of Police. (The Jewish Police were a Nazi creation, by the way—we did not have a Jewish Police force before the occupation). It is historically important to understand what the so-called Jewish Council was about, as many Jews who lived during those times hold many bad feelings about those who were on that Council, since nearly every Jewish community under German rule had one.

These councils were called *Judenrat* and made up by the most influential men from each city where they served. In simple explanation, they handled everyday business of the ghetto, much like the mayor and city council do. The problem was that they were appointed by and ruled by the Nazis. Indeed, the reason for the Judenrat was to keep havoc from occurring by the ghetto's inhabitants (or between them) and also to make sure everyone followed their orders. In this case the Nazis were smart enough to know that the Jewish people greatly resented them and so it became important for them to create a pseudo-Jewish leadership. I say "pseudo" because the members of the Judenrat were established to assist the Nazis in their need to "control" the Jewish population(s). Among the duties of the Judenrat members was to make sure that "their people" obeyed the rules, paid taxes and were put to labor. Many citizens resented this because of the blatancy of the Judenrat being an extension of the Nazi regime and accused the members of being as immoral as were the Nazis themselves. And this was true of some who actually used their political positions to line their own pockets from less fortunate Jews while gaining sanctions and other rewards from the Germans. This did not happen in every Judenrat, however, and not every member was (or became) corrupted. Yet there were enough of those council members in a number of cities who became self-serving to leave bitterness in the hearts of many Jews who suffered much agony because of them. What I believe to be the truth is that many Judenrat members in many of the ghettos and cities were conscientious and did all they could to do right under the circumstances. On the other hand, there were also those of greed and ambition who took great advantage of their positions as leaders. My conclusion, however, is that the nearer any government or governing body becomes to totalitarianism, the more naturally their members will fall into the trappings of gaining self-serving and heartless attitudes.

In any case, it was Judenrat representatives that ordered Abe and me to go to work at Kadzielnia, the stone quarry. We were paid a pittance to do so, but that was better than giving free labor at one of the camps. At least we could buy a little food and grain and that would keep us alive one day to the next; that would assist our entire family. Incidentally, while we lived in the ghetto under such stringent rules and impoverished quarters, we got to know a Nazi by the name of Hans Kessler who was with the *Schutz Polize*. He was among the few exceptions to the rule. That is, he was a German who had empathy and therefore showed Jews some kindness. In fact, he would bring us food when he could and we often communicated with him as an extended part of our family. Hans had a partner who also had an open heart and treated us with heartfelt caring, and so both these men became subtle teachers in that we realized that even some of the Nazis were surviving, too—that is, that they were "stuck" in their roles, just as we were "stuck" in ours. Not many Germans in uniform were in this category, however, especially since they had been so indoctrinated in believing that we were a tainted and sub-human people. Once a people have been dehumanized and so deemed to exist outside the sphere of humanity, it is then easy to torture and murder them without conscience. In fact, for a great many holding such authority over others, causing suffering and death becomes a rewarding experience, an act of deeply personal pleasure! And so, no, there were not many like Hans and his partner, and this is why I remember them so fondly to this day. Kindness from strangers, after all, was a rare commodity back then and when it was given, it was truly appreciated and remembered.

When I speak of acts of kindness, you must realize that I am talking about a time when millions of people were being tortured and murdered simply because they were different or held different views. Jews were the major target because they are not only a private people but their religion is intrinsic to their way of life. As a result, Jews are easily isolated and so when you add the fact that they were—as a group—made the scapegoats for Germany's economic struggles, it becomes easier to understand why they so readily became objects of hate. Hitler understood this all too well and worked hard to establish hate in the German hearts before ever stirring the German people to go to war. So combine such hate with the promise of world domination and you have created a war machine that is not only zealously obedient but mindlessly inhumane. We witnessed this inhumanity daily. Indeed, it became common to see people shot on the streets for no reason. For example, I recall one day seeing a tall man with crutches making his way to wherever he was going when a passing Nazi simply drew his revolver and shot him. He had done this murder with the ease of a person stepping on a bug without concern. These murderous acts were commonplace over those war years, and so any act of kindness toward us was engraved deeply in our souls.

Abe and I worked hard at the stone quarry and were constantly under armed guards who not only made sure that we did not run away but watched for anyone slowing down in their laboring. After all, the prisoner's only value was his labor and if he did not or could not labor well enough, then he was given no value at all.

There were two Polish workers at the quarry, Nogay and Witkowicz, who lived nearby and Witkowicz's wife would bring her husband lunch and also some for Abe and me. In exchange we gave her clothing which we brought from home. After all, we knew by eating better we were building up our bodies and this, too, would help sustain us as we continued in our quest to survive.

We were more fortunate than many living in the ghetto. As the months passed, others began dying from hunger and sickness. We had virtually nothing by then, but what little we did have was often taken by the Nazis, who would raid our houses and simply take whatever they wanted. Soon enough, there was nothing worth taking left and so we were mostly left alone to wallow in our own misery. We sometimes believed that this was how life was going to be, and so we found ways to adjust to those wretched conditions. We simply didn't conceive of the horrors that were soon to arrive.

5.

I had quite a close call while working at the quarry: I had stepped away from the worksite to talk with a few people and when I returned, a guard by the name of Novak stopped me. He gave me a resentful look and slapped me to the ground, saying he was going to shoot me. It is interesting that when a person is confronted with a truly dangerous assailant who is threatening death that both the past and future lose all meaning and only the present moment has reality. In fact, my entire reality suddenly condensed into a world that only contained the guard and me as I waited for him to pull the trigger. To this day I do not know why he didn't, but to this very day I still wonder at the fact that I am still alive anyway.

Life went on at the quarry and in the ghetto after that. Conditions continued to worsen in the ghetto for most of the inhabitants, but by and large, most of us were managing to survive and with that objective at the foremost of our minds, we had learned to live with being constantly under guard and having so much of our lives under cruel dictatorship.

We often worried more about our family members who we were separated from. Since the Germans had invaded Russia, all mail had been stopped between the two countries. As a result we had stopped hearing from my brother Seweryn, which worried my mother and, for that matter, worried all of us. We could only pray for his well being. As for my brother Moniek, he had successfully traveled to Lithuania with his bride-to-be, Rachel. As I said earlier, Rachel had family in the city of Mariampole and so we hoped that all was well there. What we didn't know was that by then the Lithuanians were supporting the German cause and a group of them, along with a group of Nazis, gathered the population of 9000 Mariampole Jews, chased them into an open field and shot them all. My brother and his bride were among them.

There were sad, troubling and frightening stories pouring in from everywhere, it seemed, and there were plenty of stories that wove through the ghetto, as well. Take Szymon's wife, Luba. Her father, Lazer Aronowicz, was a talented and hard working carpenter and only 51 years old. He came down with a sudden sickness and was gone within two weeks. Death and grief were a constant, and yet we managed to keep hope that such times were destined to pass and that we would survive them. Then one night after our talking in the evening, we all went to bed. After all, I would have to get up early the next morning for work, as would Abe and Szymon. When there is a lack of food, rest becomes an important commodity, especially for hard, manual labor as we did at the stone quarry. It was sometime in the middle of the night that, as the saying goes, *all hell broke loose.* We were awakened by machine gun fire and the blasting of grenades. Were the Germans under attack, were the Russians storming in, what was happening? Many thoughts galloped through our minds as we got to our feet, our hearts pumping from the sudden shock of it all.

We did not have to wait long to learn what was going on. Nazis entered and ordered us outside; we were going to be transported. They looked around to make sure they weren't missing anyone. We did not know it then, but Nazis had already been to the hospital, where they poisoned some patients and cut the throats of others. Whoever they found ill in bed or who had a problem walking, they murdered immediately as they continued to go from house to house, apartment to apartment, ordering people to leave their premises. There was something else—they ordered mothers to leave their babies behind before evacuating to the outside. Mothers refused to do this and so the Nazis simply shot them both.

The city was divided into three parts for deportation. We were told that we were to be traded to Russia for German prisoners. This was a lie the Nazis concocted to reduce the Jew's fear and make them more compliant to follow orders! Not following orders was to commit suicide, anyway. Our ghetto was crawling with S.S. troops, Gestapo, German police, Ukrainian and Lithuanian "Einsatz Commandos" and Polish police. This was an intimidating force to say the least, a force of murderous fiends in full uniform and quick to shoot anyone who disobeyed them.

We were divided into three groups. The first group—over 6,000 —was made to sit on the ground and give up their jewelry, watches, money and anything else of value. Thereafter they were marched to the train station, where they were stuffed into boxcars—120 human beings packed so tightly together that people could not even sit down. There was no water and no sanitary facilities; the air was thick and stale.

The second group would face the same fate a day or so later. During that time an extremely touching incident occurred. Our Rabbi, who had safely been in hiding for three years, bravely walked onto the streets of the Ghetto. He must have known that these were days of great unhappiness and loss for us Jews, as he was wearing his holiday dress, with a white shawl over his shoulders and the traditional high top hat. Behind him was a procession of many Jews, a congregation of people on a death walk. It was the stuff that causes tears in motion pictures, but there was nothing here of storytelling. This was human drama in sad and mournful motion.

Strangely enough, the Nazis did not respond as the Rabbi and those behind him passed them. His head was held high and he walked with the clarity of being leader of his community. Perhaps the Nazis and their militant supporters thought, *Those people are dead anyway; let them have their foolish march.*

I do not believe that my brothers and I surmised the actual dangers that waited for us; we probably were in the hope that we were actually being traded to the Russians for Russia's German prisoners of war. If we doubted this, we at least maintained the wishful thinking. Our parents were more perceptive. We were in the third and last wave of the deportation, just two days after the Rabbi's march. My father opened a bottle of champagne we had hidden and poured it for us. We drank "L'chaim," which appropriately means "*to life.*"

When the time to leave came on Monday the 24th, 1942, our parents handed Abe and me my mother's rings and my father's gold watch. Not wanting to worry us, they said it was a mere precaution...*just in case.* Then while Abe was packing our knapsacks my father said, *"If you don't have room for anything else, please put in my Talit and Tefillin.* This means "prayer shawl" and "phylactery." The phylactery traditionally consists of two small leather boxes containing slips of paper with scripture written on them. These boxes are worn for morning, weekday prayers as reminders of one's religious duty. These sacred things were extremely important to my father.

It was very frightening walking out of our house and onto the street that Monday morning. We were confronted with German, Austrian, Ukrainian and Lithuanian soldiers; their dominance was *sneering* in an air of aristocracy and triumph. To respond with the feelings in our minds and hearts would have meant certain death, and so we obeyed. The ego, after all, seeks survival much more than appeasement and anyway, most of our egos had been diminished long before this time.

As soon as the Nazis were confident that they had stripped us of all that was valuable, we were ordered to line up in columns of ten. As it turned out, Abe and I were on both sides of our parents. Then as we reached Okrzeja Street, a few blocks from the train station, Nazi officers pulled Abe and me out of line. The parade of others continued on, and so we were not even allowed to tell our parents goodbye.

Abe and I were made to join a large group that had also been chosen. Then we were asked for our I.D. cards. They began dividing this group, too, but as soon as I said that I worked for the stone quarry I was told that from that time on I would be working for H.K.P., a German supply house. At that point I had been separated from my brother and was feeling a nagging nausea from the stress of it all. There were so many unknowns and one's stomach filled with them. For one thing, I felt that I was never going to see my mother or father again. I tried not to think this, but I knew it in my heart and no one can escape what they know in their hearts.

I had been placed in another column from Abe, but finally he was pulled out of his group and put back into the column I stood in. He was among only around ten others, while all the rest were ordered on toward the train station. My brother Szymon could have stayed with us also, but he refused. He chose to go to the train with his wife. If she was to die, he would die with her.

We were able to watch the columns continue toward the train platform, but soon enough we were being returned to the ghetto. There were bodies lining the streets that we walked, probably those who had been shot along the way for not keeping up or stumbling or whispering. None of those who were driving the columns of people down the streets needed much of an excuse to kill a Jew.

Abe returned to work at the German factory, while I worked at the quarry. Two or three weeks had passed when a few people who had escaped the Nazis snuck back into the ghetto with their stories. It was from those escapees that we learned that our loving parents, our brother and his beautiful wife Luba had been sent to Treblinka, one of the most vicious death camps in Poland. There they made the arrivals undress and after taking everything from them, had them gassed. My parents, along with my brother and his wife, had been among them; my heart was broken.

A few months thereafter, Abe was transferred to work in a munitions factory and I was sent to Camp Bliziny. Bliziny was only around 20 miles from Kielce, a big compound that held Jews from all over Poland. This was a manufacturing camp where the prisoners were making many things for the Germans. I was sent to make canvas bags and other canvas things during the night shift.

I was miserable on the night shift. Our job was gluing together bags and the glue was so wretched smelling that it kept me on the verge of sickness. I always felt like throwing up, so finally I asked the shop foreman to transfer me. I thought I had a good chance at being transferred; for one thing, because he was Jewish and for another, I knew him. He once worked for my father, making the upper part of shoes. If anyone was to give me a break in that place, it was him...or at least, that is what I thought or hoped.

He refused me every time that I asked. I suppose he was afraid of losing his position or even being punished by the Nazis for showing favoritism, but there was something else. This was the first time in his life that he was in any kind of authority, although it was a pseudo position of power—no Jew had any real authority working for the Germans—but perhaps, even at that, keeping his ex-employer's son in line was somehow rewarding to him. On the other hand, he had been to our house many times as a welcomed friend to eat with us, so I am not certain why he refused me, but I was kept on the wretched night shift and breathing that rancid odor, a stench that was all but unbearable to me.

Anyway, there were scraps of leather and canvas that were useless and so thrown away. I would stuff my pocket full of those scraps from time to time so that I could exchange them for food with the Polish people outside the gate. One morning after my shift, I was approaching my barracks when a Ukrainian guard, in his black Nazi uniform, noticed the bulge in my pockets and stopped me. A Jew caught even putting scraps in his pocket could be shot and I realized that I had been caught. The guard looked down to my pants, where my number tag was pinned. I was number 696. He motioned me forward. I was certain that he was going to report me.

It was only a few minutes after I entered the barracks when other guards came in, hollering for number 696 and looking about for the person with that number tagged to him. I was shaking I was so nervous. Then I looked down and saw the "miracle." Somehow my number tag got turned around so that it read 969. The guards left with a shrug because they could not find 696. My life had been saved. It would not be long after this that I had another very close call, but nothing was ever as beyond understanding as my number tag getting turned upside down. I am sure that I said many prayers of thanks for having my life saved after such a close call, although I was slowly becoming bitter when it came to such things as prayer. I will talk about this a little later.

The Bliziny camp was large. There were around 2000 Jewish inmates there. The head Nazi was a man by the name of Nell. He was a

34

dangerous man who had his group of Ukrainian murderers take many into the nearby forest, where they were shot. They would be shot for not working hard enough to please some guard, for getting sick, for merely sticking things in their pockets as I had done. A person could be sent into the forest simply because a guard (or Nell) didn't like the way he looked. There were no judges or juries, only executioners. In any case, Nell was an older man—I would guess in his seventies—a cantankerous and miserable man who would strut about in his uniform with a German shepherd dog at the end of a leash. Nearly every day when we returned from work he would, along with his human watchdogs, make us come out of the barracks, line up and walk into a large open field. He did this under the pretense of making sure no one had run away, but this was merely an excuse to toss about his authority and make us suffer all the more. The entire process took about two hours—rain, shine or freezing weather. My body was usually shaking from being cold, as I only had a light jacket and, as I have said before, those Polish winters were extremely harsh.

The conditions at Bliziny were harsh regardless of the weather, and the diet was terrible for anyone, but especially for people who had to work 10 and 12 hours a day. Indeed, we were fed only once a day and our meal consisted of around an ounce of bread and some soup. The soup was made of horsemeat, which I could not eat, and so I started eating potato peels and grass to stay alive, to continue to survive.

It was during this time that I heard about a small group of prisoners who were planning their escape. I would make the decision to join them.

6.

It is difficult to describe the conditions that we lived in at Bliziny, but they were constructed to cause discomfort and pain, to add torture to our torment. The barracks, for example, were hardly fit for animals: The so-called beds were made of plywood. There were no mattresses, no blankets and no pillows. There was no heat, even in the dead of winter, and winters in Poland are freezing cold. In fact, night temperatures will often drop below 30! Indeed, I sometimes still shiver when I think of spending so many freezing-cold nights curled up as tightly as I could curl, my hands tucked between my legs for a little warmth but still shaking, my teeth chattering and hoping for sleep.

Conditions were so miserable that while I fully realized escape attempts were punished with death, as soon as I heard whispers about a plan to escape, I wanted in.

I joined the "whispers" as we slowly and cautiously created our escape plan. This was quite a chore in itself, since we never met in a group but only spoke one on one. Prisoners grouping together to have a meeting about anything was strictly taboo at the camp, so it was impossible for us to coordinate our escape route together. Instead, I would talk to one that one would talk to another, and so forth. One night as I spoke through the darkness to one of my co-conspirators, we were overheard by a person who slept near us. He was a young man around my same age! I remember his name to this day but his name is not important; what is important is that he reported me to the guards, as he was so afraid that if the Germans found out that he knew of an escape plot and didn't tell them, he would be murdered.

Did I hate the informant?

No, I understood the depth of his fear and so I did not permit myself to think of the weakness he demonstrated. As I said earlier, human action can be blocked by fear, and people often do the unimaginable when stuck in the quagmire of it. Admittedly, I was scared much of the time during my ordeals over the war years but one can overcome being scared and push forward. Fear—real fear—freezes you, so to speak, in your tracks. Fear, for example, happens to some people who want to invest in a business venture but can never muster the courage to do so; fear happens to would-be artists who can't muster the courage to put a brush to canvas or to perform on stage. It is indeed possible to be so afraid of dying that one's life becomes stagnated, like a pond of still water. Such fear happened to countless people during the Holocaust, and I witnessed it just about daily. I came close to falling into the trappings of that kind of fear when the guards came and ordered me out of the barn that night. They knew I had spoken of escape and I knew that they knew. Even the talk of escape was enough to cause your execution and many, many others had died for much less than this!

It was bitter cold out as I was marched into the early night. I imagined that I would be guided into the forest to be shot but instead I was taken to a small dugout and told to jump into it. The dugout was only around four foot square and had been used by the farmers to store their vegetables in; it was nothing more than a hole in the ground, really, with a cover. I was dressed scantily and the weather was below 20 degrees. I was shaking shivering, really—from the cold and so through chattering teeth I asked a guard if I might have a blanket. He said "no" and walked away.

One does not get comfortable confined in a dirt dugout (4' X 4') in any kind of weather but when it is that cold, such a dugout becomes treacherously cruel and torturous. Add thoughts of being shot on the following day, and you have mental and physical torment that can't be fully described. In addition to everything else, there was the chance of freezing to death, anyway, so my life looked very bleak even to make it through that night.

I believe that what I am about to say concerning the hopelessness of the above situation is worth contemplating: When you are confronted with what feels or looks like a "hopeless" situation, it becomes important to let your hopelessness go, to release it from your mind. A way of doing this is that you must first accept it or, in other words, *own it* before you can "give it up" or "send it away."

*Once you have sent it away, it has no power over you, and this is what I am getting at. You can then live through the worst of times without fear and therefore in receptiveness to all, good or otherwise. This receptiveness can be golden in very tough and horrible times. As the old song says, *Que Sera Sera (whatever will be, will be.)*

Anyway, that night was, in its way, tortuous, but early the next morning I was marched into a nearby field, as opposed to the forest. I realized then that Mincberg, the chief of the Jewish police, had somehow saved me. He had reported that I was caught with a watch, and for this I would have to take a beating, but I would live. After all, as I say, an escape attempt meant certain death; having a watch in my possession was a far lesser crime and so the whippings took place in the center of the field where other prisoners were lined up. They laid me face-down on a bench, pulled my pants halfway down and one guard sat on my feet and another guard on my upper body so I could not move. Mincberg delivered the 25 lashes and afterwards I was permitted to go back and join the line of other prisoners; I had survived once again.

How I survived Bliziny I do not know, except to say I kept "hoping." After all, I was there for many months. In fact, a few times a week the Ukrainian guards, clad in their black uniforms, would collect a group of prisoners, march them into the forest where a mass grave was already dug, and shoot them. I watched these death marches many times: There were four guards, with one in charge, and they would put the prisoners in the middle of them and walk them, in that formation, to their grave, which was a half mile or so from camp.

*This is a very vital lesson in surviving any situation that appears hopeless. By first accepting the hopelessness, you "make it yours" and so, so to speak, you own it. Upon owning it, you can cast it out of your reality and replace it with hope. While hope might not save you, it gives you the strength to endure and to push forward; to persist. I do not claim to know how it works but I believe that mysterious *law of attraction* plays a role in these circumstances. In other words *walk in hopelessness and you attract the negative but walk in hope and you attract the positive.* Perhaps this explains how I survived six horrifying years under the Nazis?

There were nearly always those who broke down mentally from the constant suffering; the stress and hunger mixed with the terrible living conditions and the labor. I am sure that any prisoner giving any signal of not coping mentally (ever as much as physically) was deemed useless and therefore destined to that forest grave. There was also the never-ending threat of a guard simply taking a disliking to you or deciding you were not working hard enough or responding fast enough to some order. Indeed, a guard not feeling well himself or who was just in a poor mood was able to vent his discomfort by taking it out on the prisoners. In this regard, we will never know how many Jews and other prisoners took beatings and/or were murdered for nothing more than an angry or upset whim of a guard or some Nazi official. As I said, we were at the mercy of these cruel and callous human beings who became the swastikas that they wore: cold and brutal living symbols of Germany's power and pomposity.

As a quick aside, the swastika was not a flash of brilliant designing genius by Hitler. In fact, the design goes back at least 3,000 years before it was ever conceived of as a symbol for the Aryan race. For ancient cultures it was used to symbolize the life-giving sun. The word itself, I am told, comes from the Sanskrit *swastika* meaning "good" and "to be," clearly a positive meaning. Indeed, during World War I the American 45th Division carried a swastika patch on their shoulders, as did the Finnish air force during the Second World War. Hitler chose it for the Nazi Party in 1920. He had written in Mein Kampf that the "new flag" had to be *"a symbol of our own struggle"* as well as *"highly effective as a poster."* Soon enough the symbol—the swastika—became associated with anti-Semitism, death and suffering. It has now been outlawed in Germany if used to symbolize Nazism, and in America the symbol is all but taboo. It is still used, however, in positive ways by religions such as Hinduism and Buddhism, and it has also been used as a positive symbol by Native Americans. Nevertheless, it was a brilliant choice made by Hitler since his flag began with a symbol that already had significance to people world-round and if not on the conscious level, then on the unconscious level in the Jungian sense. There is just no doubt about it, Hitler's madness had a genius woven through it—an evil genius, but a genius nevertheless.

Returning to Bliziny and the fourteen months or so that I somehow survived there, life and death had continued in their routines without any changes. The murder marches that occurred two or three times a week continued as the forest graves became larger, or at least more numerous, and the daily truck that came around to pick up people who had died was coming around more often as well. Many people simply were not healthy enough to make it through the harsh winters. Indeed, I sometimes wonder how anyone survived the weather being fed so little and worked so hard, but many did and I am thankful that I was among them.

Life actually got a little better at Bliziny when Nell was sent away and a younger German by the name of Kurth Heller came in to oversee the camp. His stay as commander of the camp was destined to be short-lived, however. The Germans were enduring more resistance by the Russians than they had anticipated, and the Russians were in fact closing in on those aggressors, especially near the border. Under these conditions the decision was made to liquidate our camp, with the prisoners being sent to Auschwitz.

We knew that Auschwitz was a death camp, and I believe a certain cloud of even deeper depression gathered in our heads. As I said earlier, there is no greater feeling of despair than that despair that makes you want to escape yourself. Such desperation arrives when your problems or challenges are such that you feel there is no escaping them, that you are stuck in a terrible place or position from which there is no exiting. Auschwitz, the hell of hells! After all, surviving Bliziny had been difficult enough and anyway, just staying alive as long as we had, had been nothing short of miraculous, but now...now we were going to be sent to where millions were sent only to die. It is very difficult to hold on to the *spirit* of survival under such conditions, and yet *the spirit of survival was all that we had left.* The "trick," if you will, was to find the path to exchange hopelessness for hope...Thankfully the "hope" paid off, thanks to Kurth Heller, who had some heart.

Kurth Heller took the time to write the authorities at Auschwitz that we prisoners from *his camp* were both productive and obedient.

This greatly enhanced our chances to survive, and he knew this. As I have said before, not every Nazi was the "devil" in disguise. On the other hand, most were and even worse than this at Auschwitz.

When the day arrived to leave, we were marched to the train station, given a small piece of salami and, once again, loaded onto boxcars. So many prisoners were packed so tightly in each boxcar that we had to stand all the way. Fortunately, the entire trip was only around eight hours, but those eight hours were exhausting. (Not everyone survived the trip). What also added to the misery was knowing that we were headed to an extermination camp. It isn't that we were not used to having our fate dangling from some German's strings, but we had heard horror stories about Auschwitz, and so I am sure that our hearts were pumping with a little more anxiety than usual.

The train pulled to a stop inside the camp and we were ordered out and made to stand in long lines. By then I think we were all too exhausted from the conditions of the traveling to do much thinking at all; we just lined up as ordered and waited for whatever was to happen next.

We were marched to an area of the camp called Birkanau. The barracks in Auschwitz were large and held around 60 prisoners with bunks (upper and lower), as in other barracks, with nothing on them such as blankets or pillows. We had just started to settle in when an S.S. Trooper who must have weighed at least 300 pounds marched in. He managed to stand on a stool to announce that we were all going to have a shower.

We prisoners were privy to what "having a shower meant" in the German death camps and I tried to cautiously move to the back of the line, hoping that somehow I might be saved, overlooked or missed. It was the only thing I could do to attempt saving myself. In the meantime, the fat S.S. Trooper, still balancing himself on the stool, was telling us not to be concerned, that we were not going to the crematorium but were going to have "real showers."

I did not believe him and so I continued inching my way toward the back row. After all, when it comes to surviving, it is important to always do whatever is possible to overcome the obstacles. Backing up may not sound like doing much, but it was the only thing I could think of that even *might* keep me from being murdered. After all it was impossible to run away and even more impossible to fight. And so all I could do is slowly move to the back of the line without drawing any attention to myself. *Perhaps some miracle would occur,* I hoped!

This is an important lesson, because when some people find themselves in difficult situations—even in normal life—such as terrible financial problems, they tend to fold emotionally inward and become immobile. *I just feel that I can't get out of bed,* they might say, or *I just want to sit in some corner and hide.* Well, I know these feelings all too well from my experiences during the Holocaust but I tell you, no matter how difficult your situation, you must always—always—muster the courage to do something, even if it is to talk to strangers...anything that is positive human action. In my circumstance all I could do was to slowly retreat to the back of the line but "the back of the line" was the only hope that I had.

As it turned out, the S.S. Trooper was telling the truth. However, I do not think any of us believed him until we saw the water spraying down on us. Ah, what relief! First of all from knowing that we were not being murdered—at least in those moments—and secondly, from the pure joy of feeling the water on our bodies. I had not had a shower for at least a year and a half, so you can imagine what a wonderful treat it was simply to feel clean for a change. The shower also had some kind of disinfectant in it to prevent disease, and this was good, also.

After the shower we were marched to a warehouse, where we were given some light clothing with the word "Jude" on the back of the thin jackets we were to wear. This term meant that we were Jewish, that we were the "least" in this camp of many slaves. And speaking of many slaves, the barracks that I was sent to housed gypsies only the day before we arrived. Indeed, on that particular day there were more than 20,000—yes, 20,000—gypsies murdered and taken to the crematorium.

I was told that they had not done much to resist, but how does anyone resist in such circumstances?

In speaking of non-resistance, it is interesting that when the Nazis first invaded Poland, there was a German Jew who wanted to earn favor from the invaders, and so he took them to the houses and apartments where Jewish families lived. He was with the first group of Nazis who had come to our home and stood with them as if he too were the enemy. I accidentally ran into him after arriving in Auschwitz, where he had been sent just like the rest of us. The Germans had no more respect or liking for Jews who betrayed other Jews in their behalf than they did for any of us. As I have said before, such Jews were merely used then cast aside like so much garbage, but there were still a few of those who never figured this out and attempted to win favor from the Nazis until they too were cast into the death camps.

In any case, I had arrived in Auschwitz and had survived for at least a little longer. I recall that first night lying on the wooden "cot," wondering what the next day would bring. It seemed to take a very long time to go to sleep but only moments for morning to roll around.

7.

One of the first things that happened is that I met with the infamous Joseph Mengele face-to-face. Mengele was also known as *The Angel of Death*. It is emotionally difficult for me to attempt to describe the man but I will try: He was, first of all, the ultimate Nazi. That is, his uniform was neat and spotless and his boots well attended; he wore the pomposity of his power in the very way that he walked and talked, an apparent egotist but not so obviously a psychopath. He was a psychopath, nevertheless, since no normal human being could have been as callously cruel as he was: a torturer and murderer of children as well as adults. He was young, by the way, in his mid-thirties, I would guess, or at least he looked to be around this age to me.

I will tell you a little about his work and other so-called doctors at Auschwitz, because what went on there should never be forgotten, so that no human beings will ever go through such terrible agonies again.

There was a pseudo-hospital at Auschwitz. I say pseudo because it was, in actuality, a horror chamber where inhuman experiments were conducted on people. Mengele, who is most well known for his cruelty, worked in the same facility as did others of his same mold.

There was a Dr. Carl Clauberg who was inventing a method to sterilize women en masse without the trouble and cost of surgery. In his attempts, he mixed a chemical irritant that severely inflamed the fallopian tubes, slowly causing them to grow shut. This was a very long and painful procedure that the women being used as laboratory rats endured. And by order of Clauberg, many were murdered simply to conduct autopsies on them. His ambition was to be able to be able to sterilize hundreds and hundreds of woman a day!

But why was this sterilization going to be important?

The plot was this: As Hitler's Third Reich conquered other nations, the people of those nations would be used for labor but sterilized so that they would eventually die out and Aryans would begin populating the world. While this might sound like a weird, silly plot from the pen of some science fiction writer, this plot to populate the world with only Aryans was actually on Hitler's agenda, and Clauberg was not alone in working on the mass sterilization challenge. Another *crazy* involved in this very pursuit was a Dr. Horst Schumann.

There was a Dr. August Hirt—not at Auschwitz, but at a German university—who wanted to collect Jewish skeletons in the desire to prove that his anthropological studies would produce proof that the Nordic race was superior. The "good" doctor simply requested 115 people be murdered for his purposes, and that request was quickly fulfilled.

For some, being instantly killed would have been a blessing. After all, many prisoners were taken from the Auschwitz prison camp and sent to the "hospital," where they were infected with contagious diseases for German doctors and scientists to study. Many of these "guinea pig" prisoners in fact were taken directly from the area of the camp where I was imprisoned—*the Birkanau sector!*

There are virtually countless horror stories that went on in that house of horrors called a hospital—some told, some never to be known, but all gross statements of man's inhumanity to man, all demonstrations of evils that are in the potential of *our kind*. And concerning this, many agree that the most evil was Josef Mengele, *Doctor Josef Mengele!*

Mengele's major interests were Genetics and Eugenics, with a special interest in the phenomena of twins and of dwarfism. Indeed, he would often select people with physical peculiarities who had arrived in my sector and have them taken directly to the "hospital." He would put them through a tortuous physical examination that lasted for hours, with few ever being seen again after they had served his purposes. Once inmates had served his purposes, he simply ordered them killed by phenol injection. Mengele was very apt in ordering murders, in fact. He once had a wall marked at around five feet high. All little children who didn't reach that mark in height were sent, by Mengele's order, to the gas chambers! And if a child had a specific disease, he would often have that child's head removed, preserved, and sent to institutions such as the Medical Academy in Graz, Austria. He was heartless!

One day we prisoners were in our barracks when guards entered and ordered us to undress and go outside. As soon as we were outside we were lined up and moments later, Josef Mengele was inspecting us one by one. He made each prisoner, including me, stick out their tongues and hold out their hands, palms up. Mengele and his two assistants did this as they slowly went through the rows of naked men. Upon finishing this task, Mengele stepped back from the front of the line slightly and began pointing. When he pointed his finger to the left, those prisoners were marched directly to the crematorium. When he pointed to the right those prisoners were permitted to live. I had survived one more time!

Sometime after this the Red Cross made a visit to Auschwitz. The Germans wanted the visitors to see how *"wonderfully"* we prisoners were treated and so they formed a small orchestra out of prisoners who could play instruments and gathered us around, as if this was a usual part of our entertainment. The Red Cross observed all this with a certain appreciation, as they were purposely blinded to the real conditions of the camp's prisoners.

Something I have not mentioned yet is the constant stench of the bodies being burned in the crematoriums, and this smell was in the air as the visitors from the Red Cross observed the players and listened to the music. The orchestra played two songs—My Prayer and Twilight Time—as the scent of the dead filled our nostrils. To this day, I cannot listen to either of those songs without a deep anger and depression clouding around me; to this day, I can still remember that visiting day and how utterly useless the Red Cross was. They, as it turned out, were merely passive observers and nothing more!

When I think back to that constant smell of burning bodies in the air, I am reminded of one day when I was in the barracks and guards brought in a group of around two dozen boys, all younger than ten. They were handsome and still bright-eyed, yet afraid and curious. Each

46

of the children were carrying little lunch boxes and knapsacks with food that they had brought with them from their homes. I felt gushes of empathy roaring through my body and thumping in my own heart. I wanted to ease their pain, or at least their fear, and so I attempted to speak with them. I asked them where they were from, who they were and how they were rounded up. They were all from the same small city in Poland. As they shared their story, I did my best to listen with great interest (and patience),but it was difficult because the odor from the crematorium was very thick that day and I knew in my heart within an hour or so these young, hopeful and loving boys would be gassed and their bodies burned as well. I loved each of them in that time and place, but I was helpless to save them or to save anyone, for that matter...even myself!

Something happened to me on that particular day. I had seen so much and lived through so much, and yet that day seemed to place a dark shadow in the very depths of my soul that I sometimes battle to this very day. Being with those children and knowing their immediate fate was too difficult to endure, and so I lost—or perhaps better said, "I released"—my faith in God. My question was not so unordinary as I stood isolated in a kind of existential reality asking, *If there is a God, why would he let these terrible things happen?*

I am going to talk about this *reality* a little later on in my story but at that time, I was feeling such inner rage, and that question became haunting—*if there is a God, why would he let such terrible things happen?*

Life (and death) continued at Auschwitz, and brutal rape, as well: There was a women's barracks not far from my own, and I would often see Nazi officers and other soldiers going there. They would rape the women at will and sometimes two or three men would go together, adding to their mindless games. And, now as I look back on it all, I imagine that little children often became victims of sexual crimes, too. Remember, especially Jews were soulless to the Nazis, subhuman and so of no value. They were to be used like workhorses and then killed so that food was not wasted on them. Because of all this I would sometimes think about women and children enduring the terror and torture of the German camps; I would think about the horror of it all for so many people and wonder why (and how) I had survived. I thought perhaps my parents were looking over me. My parents, as opposed to God or even the angels. After all, my faith was in such turmoil at that juncture; a faith that had once been so solid and strong had, by then, diminished and simply gone away. Indeed, that same question kept reentering my mind—*if there is a God, why would he permit such terrible things to happen?*

To be at Auschwitz or, for that matter, any of the concentration camps was to witness "terrible things," of course; unimaginable human suffering was everywhere, including in the nostrils; the stench of the dead never went away at Auschwitz! Indeed, looking back, even now after more than a half century, it seems so strange and yes, unbelievable that human beings could treat other human beings so cruelly and evilly as the Nazis and their allies did. Yet, history has filled many pages with death squads and torturers; with conquering armies and enslaved people; with human slaughters and genocides, the murder of children and rape of women— and it is still going on in our so-called "modern times." In view of all this, a new questions arrives that asks how can ordinary people who marry, raise their children, have their dreams and ambitions; who shed their tears and share their laughter as their lives unfold (as all our lives unfold) be transformed into brutal monsters as so many Germans, Slovaks, Poles, Ukrainians and Lithuanians became during those war years? As an old man who has become somewhat of a philosopher, this becomes a bewildering question for me. And so I offer this as a little food for thought: *We are all the same and it is only our differences that are apparent.* And still speaking as *an old man who has become somewhat of a philosopher,* I am convinced that if only this much was understood, then all war and much unnecessary human suffering would simply go away...

In any case, one day a group of Nazis came into the barracks and lined many of us up to have numbers tattooed on our arms. My left forearm still shows my number—B1719. Being "numbered" was a signal that we were going to be moved to another camp. However, we prisoners never knew what to expect. After all, as I have said all along, upon a whim we could have been shot or sent to the crematorium; upon a whim we could be beaten or sent to be experimented on at the *"hospital,"* as so many were. Yet being tattooed had enough promise that we were going to be living a little longer, and so we were given a kind of relief.

It was not long after the tattooing that we were packed in boxcars again. This time we were on our way to Germany, to Landsberg Am Lech, a large camp confining around 2000 prisoners. Around 99% of the prisoners were Hungarian Jews. Communication was difficult because they spoke only Hungarian and did not know the Jewish language. We were confronted by an odd irony, as these Hungarians looked down on us and treated us with disdain. I could not understand this and, to be honest, I do not understand it to this very day. In fact, there were some of these so-called "Jews" who had volunteered to join the Nazis and were actually given uniforms to wear. I can think of no uniform more ostentatious than those that the Nazis wore, and so many of those uniformed Hungarians strutted about like hateful little gods with the power of life and death at their fingertips. I remember standing in line with our pathetic little cups to be filled with soup. The Hungarian servers poured only a half cup for us. There was nothing that we could do but move on, since a half a cup was better than no soup at all.

All this ill treatment continued for a few weeks. In fact, when the Hungarians marched they would often sing anti-Semitic songs. Because of this and so much else, I cannot believe that these people were truly Jews...Perhaps they had been or perhaps they were merely decoys of some kind. I don't know. However, their attitudes did change after a few weeks. The man who served as leader of the Hungarians gave them a talking to and somehow changed their attitudes toward us. Things immediately got a little better between the Hungarians and the rest of us, and this was appreciated. (This still does not explain their earlier behavior, however. Indeed, if they really were of the Jewish religion, as they said that they were, their behavior against us still baffles me to this day).

Just being at this camp, however, was painful enough. For one thing it was late fall and the weather had turned freezing cold. We slept on plywood with nothing to cover ourselves with, so I used to worry about getting sick. I worried about getting sick because a prisoner who got sick had no chance to survive. They were simply shot!

Speaking of "being murdered," I can say that the greatest slaughters occurred in Germany in terms of individual madness. That is, a lot of truly ignorant low-lives who were gun crazy and criminally motivated had been easily recruited by the Nazis. Landsberg Am Lech had their share of this type of individual, and we prisoners did our best to stay away from them...staying away from them, as always, was our only defense. There were also treacherous guards there. I remember two who were extremely dangerous; both had been wounded fighting in Russia and had volunteered to serve at the concentration camp. One had been shot in the hand and that hand had been paralyzed from the wound. The other S.S. guard had been shot in the groin. Both reflected hatefulness in their eyes, but I personally never had a confrontation with them, as I was smart enough to avoid them whenever possible. After all, they were very cruel individuals who would murder without hesitation...and often did!

Even a few Jews who were shot served the Nazis at Landsberg. Sometimes we would see dead bodies hanging on the fences that surrounded the compound, as if those bodies belonged to prisoners who tried (foolishly) to escape. The truth was, however, that they had been shot and then draped across the wire merely to frighten the rest of us from ever attempting to escape. Nearly all we prisoners knew this but every now and then new dead bodies would be slung across the electrified fencing, and so the same ploy was repeated time and time again. By this time, there was little that the Germans could do to surprise, fool or shock me. This was nearing the end of 1944, and I had been living under their thumb for five years by then. By then my body was weakening a lot, too. I was down to "skin and bones"—our diet was a small piece of bread and some soup for the entire day—and becoming more despairing. I remember that my shoes finally fell apart at Landsberg Am Lech and I had to wrap wire around them to keep them on. I remember at least one guard having a little heart and now and then letting us go into the garbage dumps for a few minutes in order to dig out something possible to eat. The smell was so sickening that it drove me away no matter how hungry I was. I also remember wondering if I was going to survive at all. I do not mean that I had never had such thoughts before, but after five years of hard labor, malnutrition, mental anguish, heartbreak, beatings and other mistreatment, I was simply wearing out and I knew this. The S.S. troops and other guards in Germany were in some ways more hateful and callous than at other camps. It is difficult to explain how one hell can be worse than another, but at the camps in Germany there was a cruel arrogance that persisted, a kind of human ignorance pompously strutting about in S.S. costume. I cannot explain this in any other way except perhaps to say that many of the camp's staff and guards were mindless demigods who truly saw themselves as the masters of the world and Jews as no more than dirt under their feet.

Under these conditions and after going through so much, I felt that perhaps this was where it would all end for me, and I was not far from being wrong.

8.

For some unknown reason I had always been fortunate not to be chosen for the crematoriums or to be shot. I had taken beatings and been locked away in terrible solitary confinements but had been spared being made to walk to my death. Nevertheless, I had two very close calls at Landsberg.

One day two S.S. guards ordered me and a handful of other prisoners to follow them, which we did. We were marched to a small bunker that felt somewhat like a freezer from the long, winter weather. Gathered inside, we discovered ourselves with a dozen young, naked bodies of Jews. We were going to be transported with them to Dachau. This was—we assumed—a death sentence for us. We'd travel with the bodies and be gassed then cremated, too. I don't recall if we prisoners were able to talk about this but I am sure the anticipation was on all our faces. My parents must have been watching over me that day, I thought, because for some reason the order was reversed and I was able to walk away.

On another occasion I was ordered to jump into a ditch that had been dug. The ditch was 3 or 4 feet deep and I was ordered—at gunpoint—to run back and forth; an evil game of the guards and a flaunting of their power over life and death. I could do nothing but follow the order and to keep running—back and forth, back and forth. I was waiting for the sting of bullets at any moment. Indeed, by this juncture of my imprisonment I had seen others murdered just for the pleasure of some sneering Nazi, and I was in a situation where this was—with little doubt—going to happen to me. I will never, never understand why it didn't. But soon enough the guards got bored with their game and let me get out of the ditch. Even then, I was in disbelief that I was still breathing; by then I was so exhausted that, at least for the moment, I didn't really care.

I must admit that after so many years of hunger and enduring such horrifying conditions, my spirit to survive was weakening. I had been, after all, a slave of extremely cruel masters, masters who had murdered my beloved mother and father and many other of my friends and relatives, along with millions of other human beings. And my body, too, was waning in health and this, I am sure, had much to do with my mental attitude. I was, as I said, skinny as a rail, unimaginably skinny and yet I would be losing even more weight later. Indeed, as I think back to those bitter days and recall the way we prisoners all looked—gaunt, shallow-faced, down to skin and bones—I often cringe. We were, so to speak, the walking dead! It was very horrible…as I say, unimaginable. And yet, for most of us, even when the terrible gloom of existential despair possessed us, we found ways to overcome the deep depressions and give ourselves at least little glimmers of hope. Hope, faith, desire…call it what you may, but I am convinced that the want to survive alone kept us going in both a real way but also in a metaphysical way, a mind over matter way. After all, in spite of all the misery and brutality endured by all of us who were enslaved and still alive by 1944, we were a phenomenon of favorable happenstance and of unexplained blessings. And so, even to this day, I wonder about such things as how am I here? In fact, I have those moments looking in the mirror and recognizing that miracle called myself, and I become overflowing with appreciation for life and living it.

Anyway, in mid-winter at Landsberg there was a lot of activity happening at the camp. That is, the German troops and guards were very active, so we prisoners were curious about what was going on. After all, what the Nazis did always altered our fate in one way or another. Then one day the guards ordered us to leave the barracks and walk into a large open field. Once in the field we were told to wait and so we did. As we waited some prisoners died. They died from starvation and/or from sickness. And the cold air was piercing! Finally, we found out that we were being sent to different camps and I was chosen for the group being sent to Dachau, another extermination camp. At that juncture I didn't care, because just climbing into the back of the big panel truck and being shielded a little from the weather felt like good fortune.

It is somewhat interesting to me that the S.S. camp commanders were told to use their own discretion when it came to the camp's prisoners. I am supposing that by mid-1944 and early 1945 that the Nazi high command had more to think about than us Jews. And so we were left in the hands of camp leadership. As a result, we were ordered many times to simply gather outside and sit. There was no reason for this except to satisfy the S.S's sadism. The weather was freezing cold and snowy! It wasn't only that we had inadequate jackets to wear, but since we were immobile the coldness was all the more penetrating. In addition, our bodies had no fat to insulate us at all, so this was torture and this happened to us a number of times. That is, being made to go outside and just sit. The sitting was miserable enough but to sit in that freezing weather on the cold ground was simply maddening. I do not know why we did not all get sick and die, but most of us there continued to survive.

We were immediately put to work at Dachau. I did some farming and worked in the camp's lumber yard and on the railroad tracks. All this was hard labor, but at least the working kept us warmer than we would have been otherwise. By mid-April of that year, however, we noticed a lot of activity going on, just as the Germans had been so busy before abandoning Landsberg. We prisoners wondered about this but we were never told anything. However, unlike Landsberg, the guards were shooting a lot of prisoners and sending them to be cremated. We didn't know it then, but the Dachau authority had been ordered to kill us all.

By early May the S.S. troops were rounding up the last of the prisoners, and I was among them. Death was everywhere in the camp and the stench of burning bodies had been consistently in the air for weeks. During the roundup a guard happened along who was pushing a metal cart that much resembled a shopping cart. It was packed with things, and the guard looked irritated by pushing it. He spotted me and ordered me to push it for him. I didn't realize it then, but this order was going to save my life. When other guards tried to take me away, the guard with the cart insisted that he needed me and so I was left alone. This, I suppose, was the closest call I'd had to being murdered and I had

had my share of near misses. I think the guard knew he had saved my life, too, but I am not sure.

We continued on the road to Kaufering. I remember being extremely weak and hungry. In fact, I tried to eat grass along my way just to pacify the terrible pangs in my stomach. Finally when night came, I was able to reach into the cart and take a can of sardines. I managed to open the can, and I gobbled them down. They only served to upset my stomach all the more and gave me dysentery. The good news was that I had a blanket around me so that helped in keeping me a little warm. There was still a lot of snow on the ground!

While the Nazis hadn't told us anything, I realized that the way they were running about Dachau in such apparent disorder that maybe we were going to be liberated. I did not realize fully until the guard ordered me away from the cart and pushed it away himself, leaving me alone. As soon as he walked out of my sight, I knew then that I was free.

The date was May 5, 1945.

No, there wasn't any jumping about or yelling at the moon in celebration; there was nothing like this because I was too cold and too frail. I wondered if I'd come all this way only to die. I actually cannot share how I truly felt or even if I absolutely believed I was liberated. Then I was confronted by two Ukrainian guards who were also walking on the road. I feared that they would shoot me but instead, they yanked the blanket away from me and continued on. I hated them in that moment and I think that all my hate manifested then as I felt it in the totality of my consciousness—how could they steal my blanket? That was my blanket!

Those moments of intense anger and hate dissipated as I continued on my way. After walking for awhile I saw an old Jewish man sitting on the side of the road beneath a blanket. I spoke to him in Yiddish, asking him if I might share the blanket with him.

The old man was very kind but also very sick. In fact, he called me by name, thinking that I was someone he knew. I said nothing to change his mind. I think he might have been hallucinating, but I am not sure. No matter, I was extremely grateful to him and the blanket kept us both much warmer than we would have otherwise have been. I would survive the night.

The next day, outside a town called Waldheim, I passed a farmhouse where a woman was boiling potatoes to feed the animals. I tried to grab a potato from the pot but the water was too hot so I finally walked away. As I did I spotted a broken branch on a tree and managed to break it off to use as a cane to support my body. I could hardly stand on my own two feet by then.

I decided that I could not walk anymore and so I managed to go into the barn, where I'd be out of the cold and could get some rest. I hoped that rest would recuperate me enough to be able to walk again. I had little idea of where I was going at that point…just away from the Germans, I suppose. I was much sicker than I knew!

I don't recall much about that night in the barn. I must have had all kinds of thoughts running through my mind and I doubt if my liberation was fully realized—one does not just recover from six years of that kind of enslavement in a few moments or a few hours or days. Indeed, I suspect that one doesn't recover fully even in a lifetime. In fact, it is not really possible to describe the horrors of the holocaust that we prisoners endured. For one thing, memories of the more hideous experiences are buried too deep into the psyche to recall. Indeed, some of the sharing that I have done so far has been difficult for me to think about, much less to share. Thinking back to my beloved parents is perhaps the most difficult of all.

Anyway, that difficult night in the barn also passed by. I think that once I was able to fall asleep, I slept very soundly. I was exhausted, after all! Early the next morning, however, one of the German women from the farm house walked across the field and into the barn to tell me that the Americans had arrived. I was so weak by then that I had to struggle to get to my feet, but I managed to hobble through the barn and go outside. I could hardly walk, so I half-dragged myself toward the tanks. I only weighed around 60 pounds by then. Yes, that's right, 60 pounds, so my weakness made even crawling challenging. As soon as the Americans saw me, they called an ambulance. I wanted to share my heart with them in those moments but I could hardly speak and they said nothing to me. They just put me in a Red Cross ambulance and rushed me to the hospital.

Two days later, as I lay in a Schwabing Hospital bed in Munich, the war in Europe ended and Hitler was dead. While the Americans, the Russians and their allies were celebrating victory I was, too, in my own way. Well, that is, I was so frail and near death by then I was not jumping up and down, but I felt a wonderful peace in my heart and that peace filled me with a joy that I cannot describe. There is something else—at that point survival would take on a whole different meaning for me. After all...I was free!

9.

I was in the Munich hospital for a few months—I still could not walk. My body was so ill and worn out. Nevertheless, the Catholic Nuns who were nurses there were wonderful; I was not used to such caring and kindness. Then I was sent to Kempten, the very hospital that treated Nazis during the war. After Kempten I was transported again, this time to a convalescent home by the name of *Bad Worishofen.

My stay at the hospitals and finally at the convalescent home were comforting, especially once I began to recover my strength. What I mean by this is the kindness I was shown by the nurses and doctors. I cannot tell you what it felt like to simply hear kind words. Words are very important and much more powerful than most people realize. To say *I love you,* for example, has the power to heal the wounded heart, just as to say *I hate you* can break a heart; to tell a person that he or she can succeed sometimes brings magic into the life of that person, just as telling a person that he or she is a failure can create failings in that person. The nurses kept telling me that I would be fine...and I believed them!

During my recovery at the convalescent home, we were visited by a Jewish group of women volunteers. The group's name was Hias and Joint Distribution Organization and the uniformed ladies gave us toiletries, clothes to wear and some money. These were treasures at the time, not to mention that the helping hands also filled us with enthusiasm for the future. "The future" is something that we prisoners of concentration camps had done without for a very long time. At first, the thought of hopeful tomorrows seemed foreign to us. After all, we were used to thinking in terms of *what would happen next* and wondering if we would be among the murdered in virtually every moment.

*The term bad in English means the opposite of good but in German the word can be interpreted as "resort."

But now that we were free again, our lives were going to be our own. I cannot tell you what a joy it is to *own* one's life again after having it possessed by such cruel and unmerciful tyrants, Devils all! But in order to survive one learns to put those sour memories behind and attempt to look only at bright tomorrows.

CHARLES' HIGH SCHOOL SENIOR CLASS PICTURE
Kielce, Poland 1938
CHARLES IS IN 2nd ROW, 3rd FROM LEFT

MOSES ISAAC PIASECKI

SZYMON (CHARLES' BROTHER) AND HIS WIFE LUBA

CHARLES - 1946

CHARLES AND HIS BROTHER SEWERYN – 1946

ABE (Charles' Brother), SALA (Abe's wife) -1945

CHARLES (RIGHT) AN USHER AT
HIS COUSIN'S WEDDING - 1953

CHARLES AND LIBBY (SEATED ON LEFT)
AT COUSIN'S WEDDING – 1953

ESTHER AND HERSHEL PIASECKI
CHARLES' PARENTS

THE UNITED STATES OF AMERICA

ORIGINAL
TO BE GIVEN TO
THE PERSON NATURALIZED

No. 7389332

Petition No. 522902

Personal description of holder as of date of naturalization: Date of birth October 19, 1920; sex Male
complexion Medium; color of eyes Brown; color of hair Brown; height 5 feet 10 inches;
weight 148 pounds; visible distinctive marks Tattoo left forearm
Marital status Married; former nationality Poland
I certify that the description above given is true, and that the photograph affixed hereto is a likeness of me.

Charles Pierce
(Complete and true signature of holder)

UNITED STATES OF AMERICA
EASTERN DISTRICT OF NEW YORK } ss:
Be it known, that at a term of the _____ District _____ Court of
The United States
held pursuant to law at _____ Brooklyn _____
on November 11th, 1954 the Court having found that
CHARLES PIERCE
then residing at 362 Linden Blvd., Brooklyn, New York
intends to reside permanently in the United States (when so required by the
Naturalization Laws of the United States), had in all other respects complied with
the applicable provisions of such naturalization laws, and was entitled to be
admitted to citizenship, thereupon ordered that such person be and is hereby
admitted as a citizen of the United States of America.
In testimony whereof the seal of the court is hereunto affixed this 11th
day of November in the year of our Lord, nineteen hundred and
Fifty-Four and of our Independence the one hundred
and Seventy-Ninth.

Charles Pierce
Seal

It is a violation of the U.S. Code (and
punishable as such) to copy, print, photograph,
or otherwise illegally use this certificate.

_____ Clerk of the U.S. District Court.
By _____ Deputy Clerk.

DEPARTMENT OF JUSTICE

CHARLES' CITIZENSHIP CERTIFICATE – 1954

66

CHARLES AND LIBBY WEDDING JUNE 13, 1954

CHARLES AND LIBBY – 1954

NIAGRA FALLS HONEYMOON

ABF (CHARLES BROTHER) 2009

TATTOO ON FOREARM

CHARLES AND LIBBY 2009

INTRODUCTION: PART TWO

I am sometimes asked how I survived those six years under the brutality of the Nazis and their advocates, the very hopelessness of the conditions I lived through hour after hour and day after day with death and the dying all around me. I will answer this question the best that I can.

First of all I saw my captors as devils and so I was living in a hell on earth. I gave myself no thoughts about the world outside the tormenting realm of that hell that I among so many others was enduring. I lived mostly in the moment, as that was my fate at the time. That is, I did not permit myself to think such thoughts such as, *when I make it through all this, I will start over and meet a nice girl and live in a nice house and have plenty to eat and sleep in a warm bed.* Such thoughts are of value only to those who have some sort of control over their own lives. In the concentration camps, we prisoners were constantly in jeopardy of being murdered and we saw others being murdered daily in places such as Auschwitz and dying of starvation and illness. In our hell, death and suffering was a continuum! Indeed, even to this day I cannot share all the terror and horror of those places, as I have buried some memories so deeply in my psyche that I am unable to summon them to the surface. I suppose I did think of the past now and then, of my parents, my brothers and life in Kielce as it once was. But such thoughts did not linger in my thinking. For one thing, those kinds of thoughts served only to drive a person mad and simply holding on to one's mind, under those wretched conditions, was challenging enough. After all, our minds were all that we had, since our bodies were under those devils' domination.

Surviving, then, is to essentially live from one moment to the next, to live in the here and now and avoid all contemplation of the then and there. As a result, it was important to let loose or, in other words, release all one's yesterdays and tomorrows, to live in the present and not permit memories or hope of better times to torment you. Indeed, the "trick" was to accept whatever came and then, if possible, to survive another day. When things in life seem absolutely

71

hopeless, then it becomes vitally important to muster the courage to just let things unfold as they will and be receptive to them. I cannot explain this but *receptiveness* seems to sometimes work miracles when it comes to positive outcomes. I offer this only as food for thought.

So yes, that I survived at all was—at least in part—miraculous. But also, as I have said before, I became the *"good slave"* without ever taking on the nature of the slave and this too was intrinsic of how I survived the Nazis and those long years of the Holocaust! Survival, however, has many faces, and this is what I want to talk about next: After recovering and walking out of Bad Worishofen, I was at long last free again. While I probably didn't realize it then, now (as an older man who has become somewhat of a philosopher) I can tell you that when we think of survival, we usually think of *surviving terrible times, times that are difficult, dangerous or tragic.* In life, however, we must also survive our freedom. As I see it, this is a most important observation.

The results of our lives, after all, are a continuous line of *chain events.* Every single choice that we make adds a new link, no matter how minor or major. Indeed, you will hear certain people saying such things as *I just don't know how I ended up in these terrible circumstances.* They do not understand (or want to) when I say, *You are where you wanted to be.*

In regard to the above, just think of how differently things might have turned out if my father had made the choice to leave Kielce before the occupation, as opposed to staying in the hope that somehow *all would be just fine.* In this regard, remember my brother Seweryn, who decided to leave Kielce and take his chances with the Russians. His life was hard in Russia, but he escaped the Nazis and the concentration camps. But what of my brother Moniek making the choice to go to Lithuania with his lovely bride-to-be? Both ended up murdered! Different choices, different consequences!

Do not take me wrong. I am not saying that it is possible to foresee the results of every decision that we make, only that each of our decisions lead us to different destinations. Take the boy who dreams about being a great violinist but chooses not to practice, or the person who dreams of being in business for himself but fails to save his money or the girl who has dreams of becoming an astronomer but decides to drop out of school...in the end we are all victims or victors of our own choices. This is what I am talking about and this is the challenge of being free!

I will never forget the day that I walked out of Bad Worishofen. To be outside and breathe air that did not have the stench of burning bodies was a certain ecstasy; to walk where I wanted to walk and not be ordered about by armed assassins felt more like a blessing than even a privilege. What I am trying to say is, on that day, I understood the richness of simply breathing free air and having the volition to walk where I wanted to walk. There was something else: My world was at peace again. There is, after all, such a cruelness to war. Indeed, there is no louder declaration of man's inhumanity to man than...the war cry!

All war in essence (and historically) is about expansionism and building treasures for the aggressors. These were the goals of Attila the Hun, Alexander the Great, Julius Caesar, Genghis Khan and Adolph Hitler. Our human history lists thousands of warmongers seeking wealth and world power who were nearly always clad in the costumes of ideologies. But all warmongers, in order to be effective, must first create fear and hate in their own populations and then dehumanize the enemy so that they will be properly despised. Hitler was a master at this—he worked years to indoctrinate the citizens of Germany into blaming the Jews for their poverty and then stir enough hate to slaughter them, to create a wide gap between who they called us (the Germans) and them (the Jews) and all others who were deemed subhuman and so intolerable.

I do not think that I had any such thoughts the day I left Bad Worishofen but I have now had many years to dwell on such things. What should be intolerable, of course, is hate itself and especially the hating of another because he and/or she is different. In regard to all this, I wish to share something both profound and beautiful with you. In order to do so, I will share the words of Joshua Loth Liebman who said:

A love of neighbor manifests itself in tolerance not only of others, but what is more important, of the essence and uniqueness of others, when we subscribe to that religious philosophy of life which insists that God made each man and woman an individual sacred personality endowed with different needs, hungers, dreams. This is a variegated, pluralistic world where no two stars are the same and every snowflake has its own distinctive pattern. God apparently did not want a regimented world of sameness. That is why creation is so manifold.

With all these thoughts in mind, I will now return to my story. After all, when I finally left the convalescent home I had the entire world before me. I was, after all, a free man.

10.

With the small amount of money the volunteers had given me, I was able to sleep in an inn after being released from the convalescent home. It seemed peculiar to be walking about in the world and doing things like a real human being again. The act of simply walking into an inn on my own volition and paying for a place to sleep—with a soft mattress, pillow and cover—was a happy reminder that the terrible times were actually over and a new life was unfolding for me.

But that happiness was short-lived. After all, I was soon enough thinking about my poor parents and the terrible fate that they must have endured. While I didn't know it then, my brother Moses had been murdered in Lithuania. My brother Szymon was dead too. He could probably have saved his life had he permitted himself to be sent to the work camps with the rest of us, but instead he had gallantly chosen to go with his wife to the Treblinka death camp where she was being sent. All in all, I had lost around 300 members of my family to the Nazi death squads and death camps. Some I had been very close to and others I did not know so well, but my entire family was nearly *"wiped out"* during those terrible war years.

During my very short stay at the inn I met other concentration camp survivors, and we talked. Everyone was hoping to find loved ones such as relatives and friends, and so we did our best to share information. I was fortunate in that someone knew my brother Abe and told me he was indeed alive and living somewhere in Germany. I was grateful to have learned this and became anxious to see my brother again...*wherever he might be.* I began hitchhiking all over Germany in my quest to find him.

Along my way I met other survivors and as good fortune would have it, I was told by a couple of those survivors where I could find my brother. He was with his wife in a small mountain community called Mitenwald. I immediately set out for Mitenwald and reached the town both by hitchhiking and by train.

Mitenwald is snuggled at the foot of the Bavarian Alps, a beautiful place surrounded with majestic snow-capped mountains that seemed, to me, to be leaning against crystal clear skies when I arrived. I was a little overwhelmed by the sheer beauty of the place, but my heart was pumping with anxiousness to see my brother again. I quickly discovered that he and his wife Sala had a room in someone's house. He too had been helped by Hias and Joint Distribution, those uniformed ladies who worked so hard to assist survivors of concentration camps. Abe was staying in a house, incidentally, that was owned by royalty and a woman who had risked her life by permitting a Jewish girl to hide there. The woman had certainly been a brave friend of the young girl, especially since the Nazis despised anyone who helped a Jew as much as they hated Jews themselves. (There were many unsung heroes who did, however, and I am often saddened that their courage will never be publicly acknowledged).

The union was warm and, at times, extremely emotional. After all, we talked about old times and being with our beloved parents; we reminisced life before the war and yes, we talked also about some of the horrors that we had endured. It is a little strange, I suppose, but talk of experiencing the death camps was very sparse. For one thing, our tragic stories remained reflected in our eyes and for another, our stories were unbearable to discuss. Sala, Abe's wife, had been through her share of hell as well. And so we all celebrated our being together and being alive in our hearts. We had, after all...survived.

After I stayed around a week at Abe's I decided to remain in Mitenwald for a short time longer and took a room for myself. Ironically, it was in the house of a former Nazi, a woman by the name of Von Bentheim. Later I was lodged in a hotel where we ate. There were around forty of us and the food was supplied by the ladies of Hias and Joint Distribution. The hotel, incidentally, had formerly been owned by another Nazi whose name was Von Billof. Despite it all, my stay in Mitenwald was pleasant—sometimes very happy but also sometimes very sad. It depended on what Abe and I talked about: Speaking of our parents and brothers who had perished during the war always left both of us with lumps in our throats.

I decided that I wanted to find my brother Seweryn. We did not know at that time if he was alive or dead, but I was determined to know the truth of it. Once again I would go by train and also hitchhike as I traveled through Bavaria and the rest of Germany asking questions all along my way. During my travels I heard that my brother had returned to Kielce, our hometown, so I turned into the direction of Poland.

You must remember that I was traveling without papers during all this time and that moving about Europe was not at all like moving about the United States. In fact, I was destined to become a prisoner again, which I will talk about in the next chapter. At this juncture, I will share my narrow escape of being arrested and sent to Siberia.

Realizing that I could not enter Poland without papers, some word of mouth led me to meeting a man that could help me cross the border. I would have to pay him, so fortunately I had some money. This man and the train conductor were in cahoots and so I was directed to board a particular car and hide amidst the luggage that was inside. The other part of the direction was not to make any noise—indeed, not to make a sound. I readily agreed!

Hiding amidst the luggage was far from a comfortable trip and yet it was pure luxury compared to being boarded onto boxcars packed with people. From this point of reference I actually enjoyed the ride. I was anxious to reach Poland and Kielce to find my brother. I also had thoughts that were both negative and positive about seeing my hometown again. In some ways I almost feared returning to Kielce, since to me it held the memories of a family life and good times with so many who were by then murdered and in mass graves. That thought sickened me, and so I tried to think of other things; I tried to look forward and not back. That is a challenging task, however, especially when your parents keep popping into your mind and you imagine the horrors that they must have gone through before their deaths. That is a challenging task when you know so many that you loved are gone forever from the very town you are returning to. Even to this day, I sometimes fail to keep such thoughts out of my consciousness. This book, for example, is not an easy chore for me!

It was nice just to listen to the wheels of the train rolling along its route; those wheels sang of my renewed freedom in many ways and so I listened to them often. They often came to a halt as the train stopped to permit passengers to board or disembark at stations. At those places, the baggage car that I was in had a particular silence that was also appreciated. All in all, the trip was very favorable with one exception: At one station Russian authorities boarded the train to search it. I knew that if I were caught I would be arrested and transported to some labor camp or be sent to Siberia. For this small infraction of the law, my life could be ruined for many years, if not forever...and I knew it.

My guardian angel must have been working overtime because I was not discovered. I rejoiced at hearing those wheels start turning again. And their *"song of freedom"* sounded all the more profound to my ears. I exhaled many breaths of relief as we traveled on.

Arriving in Kielce, I felt an anxiousness roaring through my stomach; my heart beat with anticipation. Anticipation of what, I did not know beyond the possibility of seeing my dear brother again.

I walked the streets seeing, as the song says, *those old familiar places,* and my head flooded with memories—good and bad! The town itself felt like a graveyard. Certainly it had all the scars of war revealed in the debris of brick, wood and mortar that lined many of the streets in chaotic piles like memorials to tragic times. I tried to keep my mind on finding Seweryn.

I managed to talk to a few people and learned that my brother had moved to another city. What had happened—and you must know that this is after the war; this was 1946—is that a group of Polish terrorists claimed that the Jews had kidnapped a little boy and called a meeting between themselves and the Jews to discuss the alleged crime. There was no discussion on their agenda. Forty-two Jews showed up and forty-two Jews were murdered. Luckily, Seweryn had not gone to that meeting. During my short stay in Kielce I managed to visit the apartment house where I lived as a child. The visit was nothing like I thought (or hoped) that it might be. The people there were cold and

78

unfriendly, so I continued my searching for Seweryn. I would discover that he had moved to Wroclaw.

I made my way to Wroclaw without incident. Wroclaw, unlike Kielce and so many other places, did not show signs of the war. In fact, it looked safe and historically handsome, with people going about their business as if a war had never occurred. I was a bit amazed, if not overcome by it all. This is not to say that Wroclaw did not see a few tragedies of their own but the city itself was left intact; there had been no bombings and it was quite beautiful.

I had few problems finding Seweryn. He was in fact living with the same family that he had gone to Russia with, the Gringras! They had also been prisoners together but as I have said before, the Russians did not murder their prisoners, and so after six years of enslavement in Uzbekistan they survived and were finally released.

The reunion was filled with both joy and sorrow. And the Gringras were doing financially well again. They even had a maid. I stayed with them for a few weeks. We ate well and slept in comfort. Also, the weather was beautiful. As a point of interest, winter and summer, Wroclaw is considered one of the warmest places in all of Poland. In any case, before I left Seweryn tried to convince me to stay and join the Polish army. The last thing I wanted to do was to join the Polish army and so I chose to leave, regardless of his well-intended enthusiasm for me to become a soldier.

Upon my decision to leave, I knew that I would never return to Poland. There were just too many sad memories there, memories that I wanted to diminish in my psyche so that I could survive them and build myself a life. My first goal was to return to Germany, but thoughts of going to the United States were also on my mind. At that time, I did not know a lot about the United States except from stories that I had heard both before and after the war. But this, added to the fact that it was the American troops who saved me on that wretched day when I barely had the strength left in me to crawl, became very enticing. In America, I knew I could be free forever and make something of myself! Still, at that juncture of my life, I remained far more lost than found. That is, I was still in recovery from experiences in the Holocaust, so I probably wasn't half as solid-thinking as I presented myself to be. Indeed, I was still on somewhat of a bizarre merry-go-round, although I didn't realize it at the time. At the time, I felt very secure inside and so *"in control"* of my destiny.

Still without papers, I was directed toward a smuggler whom I was told would get me back onto German soil. His fee was forty dollars! I paid him and we agreed to meet later, after he had had time to make arrangements.

We were to meet at a particular hotel in the lobby. I could hardly wait! When the time came I arrived filled with anticipation and excitement but my "contact" never showed up—it had all been a scam! I was stuck in Poland at that juncture and would have to find some alternative if I was going to be able to return to Germany. For the moment I felt disappointed and yes, angry at the man who had conned me out of my money. After all, what little money I had in my pocket at the time was my only wealth. In any case, I remember my disappointment and sitting in the hotel's lobby wondering what to do next.

11.

It took only a few days before I heard of another smuggler, and this one was recommended by people I trusted. When I met the smuggler he, himself, assured me that he was honest and would indeed help me cross the border...he wanted to be paid, of course.

When we met again, the weather had turned very nasty that day, very cold. Nevertheless, I followed him to a river and he pointed out the spot that I was to cross. There was no bridge and I had no idea how deep the river was. It didn't matter; I was determined and anyway, my smuggler "friend" had quickly disappeared leaving me on my own.

I carefully scanned the wooded area across the river from me but saw no one. I also carefully looked about my side of the river to make sure that I was not being watched by anyone. I glanced at the sky, a current of gray storm clouds. I glanced back at the river, a flow of freezing cold water. I stepped in. Soon enough the water was up to my neck; the river was much deeper than it had looked from the banks. I made it across just fine, though, and when I did I was greeted by two ladies who helped me onto the bank. They had been waiting for me all along!

I was wet and so freezing cold that I could hardly do anything but shake so they took me under my arms—one on each side of me—and walked me to their house, which was only around a quarter of a mile away.

As we approached their house, I noticed that there were winter crops growing in the fields, so I had arrived in Czech farmland. The house itself was a private home with a second story. Under different circumstances the scene would have been quite enchanting to me but as it was, all I wanted was to get inside where I would be warm...and dry.

As soon as we were inside I was directed where I was to sleep (a room all of my own) and given clean clothing to wear. I immediately took a nice, hot shower, put on the dry clothing and went downstairs.

I will never forget my stay with these ladies. They were kind and welcoming, not only making sure that I felt comfortable in their home but that I was truly welcomed there; that I could relax for a change and was among friends. None of their courtesies went unnoticed by me and in fact meant very much to me. I had seen so little human kindness back then, and this house radiated with it. This house was a *home filled with love* and such loving people. While I might not have seen it quite like that while I was there, this observation is very clear to me looking back on it now. Those ladies had big hearts, and I will never forget them. Indeed, the first evening there we had a wonderful meal sitting at the kitchen table. Most of the conversation was about me. That is, the ladies wanted to know where I was from and about my family; where I was going and what would I be doing with the war ended.

I answered all the questions the best I could and told them that my major goal then was to find as many of my relatives as I could. I of course told them of my success in finding Abe and Seweryn. I also told them that I was sure that my beloved parents had been murdered but that one carries in their souls the dim hope that maybe, by some miracle, they were still alive.

I think we all knew that such hope is a "dim light" that it burns out in time and of course it did. On the other hand, I think holding on to the possibility of miraculously finding my parents alive helped me cope with knowing the truth. But surely, down in the depths of me, I knew that my parents were (no doubt) gone...forever.

The next morning, after a fine breakfast, I decided to take a walk, which I did. One of my motives was to find the best path to the German border. While I walked, I met other Czechoslovakians along my way. They were all very friendly and when I asked directions to one place or another, they not only gave me directions but walked with me to make sure I would find my way.

I stayed three days at the farm house, and on the fourth I found my way to the German border, where a Russian woman was in charge of the guards. I was able to talk with her in Polish and explained that I was looking for my family. She permitted me to cross the border and I was extremely grateful, since her decision could have easily gone the other way. I managed to get a ride on a truck and rode around five miles to the local railroad station. I bought a ticket to Mitenwald because I knew Abe would be there. I was anxious to see him again.

While I was visiting Abe I heard that there were some people from Kielce in Passau. Hoping that they might have news or information about my family members, I immediately left Mitenwald, wanting to find them.

After reaching Passau, it did not take me long to find out where people were living that were known to have moved into town from Kielce. My heart beat with excitement as I was thinking that perhaps someone was there that I had known, a friend or, yes, even a relative? I hurried down the streets to the address given me, a two story apartment house!

I knocked on doors asking questions. I was not greeted with the friendliness that I had hoped for; there were no open arms in Passau. In fact, just the opposite: As I talked to people about my history and explained I was seeking relatives that might have survived, an *old woman (a busybody) who lived on the second floor was running to the police to report me for being a stranger.

This was just to cause trouble for me, but I will never know why. Maybe she was a Jew hater and heard that I was a Jew and not a Pole from Kielce? Maybe she believed that she gained some sort of favor by informing the authorities (there are many people like this in all places) or maybe she was simply a nosy troublemaker? I will never know. All I

---

*The way that I found out that it was the old woman who lived on the second floor is that the detectives actually told me this during my arrest at the apartment house.

know is that I was quickly confronted by detectives, asked for my papers and so forth then taken off to jail.

Being arrested is one thing but being arrested and imprisoned so soon after spending a half decade as a prisoner of the Nazis is something else. That is, there is both an unconscious fear of being a captive again and a conscious fear of being at the mercy of authority. These two fears toss about in the middle of one's stomach and make the heart beat faster. Nevertheless, I succeeded in not revealing these feelings of fright that I was enduring to the police. I was too seasoned as a prisoner not to know that a show of weakness and fear is invariably misused by those in power. And so, as a result, I simply calmly followed instructions during the entire process of my arrest, part of which was to turn over everything in my possession to the police.

After being processed into the jail I was walked up three flights of stairs to my cell. The cell was small with a toilet, a small sink and three cots. There were two other prisoners already serving time there when I arrived. They were both German men, but if they ever said why they were there I do not recall the reasons. Actually, I think my body went into some kind of shock from the experience of being locked up again and all kinds of thoughts rambled through my head: *Was I going to end up leading the kind of life that Victor Hugo patterned for Jean Valjean in Les Miserables?* After all, I had no idea how long the authorities could hold me or, for that matter, even why I was being held...It was just very nerve-racking to think of my life being back in the hands of Germans. You, the reader, can imagine why I would feel this way and why it didn't matter if these were Passau Germans or not. *After all, all I knew is that I was a Jew in Germany and caged again; enslaved as far as I was concerned.*

The food was not very tasty but it was a lot better than we were given in the camps and we were taken out of our cells once a day in order to exercise. The days dragged by! What I was unaware of, however, is that when Abe did not hear from me, he quickly became concerned and began tracking me down. Fortunately, he managed to find out where I was and what had happened. He hired a lawyer who accused the police of false arrest, and I was released after two weeks of incarceration. Incidentally, I never met, spoke with or once saw the attorney who had won my release, but I am grateful to him to this very day. I am also greatly appreciative for my brother's concern and efforts to have me freed. Who knows what would have happened without their help?

In any case, the police gave me back my belongings and simply sent me on my way. I remember walking out of the police building (the jail) and feeling my entire body relax. It had been such a terrible ordeal. While I do not clearly recall my thoughts during the time I had been locked up, I must have thought about the Czechoslovakian people who had been so kind and generous to me. Indeed, to this day, I believe that the Czechs are among the nicest and most conscientiously caring people in the world. I think, too, that I thought more and more about America while sitting behind Passau bars. I remembered that it was American soldiers that freed me from the Nazis but also, I had heard stories of life in the United States and of being free. Nothing sounded more appealing than this as I endured the anxiety of being trapped in jail.

Once out, I left town as soon possible and returned to Abe and Sala's, where I would feel welcomed and safe. It is difficult to explain, but once you have been arrested for virtually no reason and jailed merely because those in charge have the power over you to lock you away in a cell, you begin living with a shadow over your shoulder, a feeling that your freedom and your life can, at any moment, always be snatched away by the mere whim of authority. Perhaps my fear was greater because of my enslavement during the war but my yearnings to go to America became very strong. As a result I wrote my Aunt Bluma, who was living in Brooklyn, New York and asked if she would sponsor me so that I could come to the United States.

As an aside, my father's brother, Isidore, and Aunt Bluma had moved to America before the war. They lived in the same building located at 1085 Eastern Parkway in Brooklyn. Uncle Isidore was married to Helen and they had a boy and a girl. He was an artist, a painter who did mostly portraits for a living but also was quite a talented painter of scenery as well. Bluma and her husband Morris had six children—*five girls and one boy!* Morris was a furrier and at the time furriers were highly respected and paid a respectable wage. Uncle Morris needed a good wage to support his large family!

I was thrilled and excited when Aunt Bluma wrote me, saying that she would sponsor me and do what she could to help me move to the United States. I could stay with her and Morris, she said, and so I would not have to worry about finding a place to live once I got there.

I was ready to go, at least in my heart, but it would take over a year for my papers to be approved. And Aunt Bluma had to pledge to be responsible for me and to help find work. I was (and remain) grateful that she was willing to make that pledge.

I also wanted to move from Abe's because I did not want to be a burden on him or his family; he had already helped me so much. In fact, who knew, if it were not for my brother Abe maybe I would still have been in jail. That thought and the thought of being arrested again often gave me anxiety. I sometimes felt very impatient to be on my way to a land that upheld laws and treated people justly. Bureaucracy is bureaucracy, of course, and there was no rushing the system that would eventually permit me into the free world. After staying at Abe's for a couple of months, I moved out to be on my own again. And again I was helped by those uniformed ladies representing Hias and Joint Distributions. They were a *godsend* to many of us who had made it through the concentration camps and were starting our lives again...penniless. There were also great lessons to be learned from that group's generosity and openness to others. Indeed, for myself, I was reminded of the wisdom from the Talmud that says, *"If I am not for myself, who will be for me? But if I am for myself only, who am I?"* (I have done what I can to live this wisdom in my life and I hope that I have taught my children the same thing; it is a good and wise philosophy and so I will repeat it: If I am not for myself, who will be for me? But if I am for myself only, who am I?)

At long last my papers were approved and I was going to be leaving for America. The relief was overwhelming, the joy cautious—

after all, what if something went wrong? I had nothing to worry about, but I did not know it at the time and anyway, I was not used to the world being on my side, so I was a little nervous until I was actually on my way.

The ship that I boarded with many other "refugees" was named the USS General W. G. Haan. She was a large transport ship built for the Navy during the war but transferred to the U.S. Army in 1946. She was 522 feet 10 inches long and could accommodate nearly 4000 troops. I was given quarters on the lower deck with several others, where we slept on cots. The food, incidentally, was excellent and plentiful— prepared by Army chefs—but I would not be eating much of it.

It seemed that the moment we were out to sea, a terrible storm brewed and soon enough the ship was rocking and being tossed about in such constant motion that I became immediately sick, far too sick to eat or to even want to see food. Seasickness can be devastating for some people and unfortunately, I was one of them. I remember, too, having to go to the bathroom and not being able to find it. Because of a language barrier I had to point in order to explain "my need" and although that was a little embarrassing, I gratefully made the emergency.

The storm lasted day after day and the seasickness stayed consistent, but I accepted it in good humor since I kept my mind positive and on the hope of my new life; I was in fact inspired, since the future looked and felt so bright after having so many years of terrible gloom. Indeed, even life after the war had been challenging and at best, trying, and so thoughts of being fully liberated pounded in my heart and I thought about this as the ship struggled through the stormy weather toward its destination...*my destination!*

I remember meeting a fellow, an American soldier, during the voyage who spoke a language that I could understand. At that juncture of my life I was not able to speak or understand English but I spoke Polish, Jewish and German fluently and also knew a little Hungarian, Russian and Italian. In addition, while in school I had done well in Latin, too, but I had never been around English speaking people so I was pleased to be able to converse with the soldier. He told me that in civilian life that he made signs for the roads and this was something that I might want to look into when I arrived in "the States." I will always remember him reaching in his pocket and giving me a dime for good luck. It was my first American coin, so it held all kinds of value for me: a symbol of better times ahead!

At long last the ship docked in Boston Harbor. I remember looking into the distance, my first view of the United States. I do not recall what was going on in my mind when I walked down the gangplank as I disembarked the ship. Once on solid ground though, I fell to my knees and kissed the ground. I could not help myself; I was compelled!

I will do my best to share that compulsion: Unless you have been enslaved you cannot know what freedom means to the heart and mind of someone that has been, someone whose life belonged to others. I realized in that moment that I had entered a land where I would belong to myself. Think on that for a moment—the very wealth of simply owning yourself! I remember kissing the ground, thinking too of my appreciation for the President and all the soldiers of the U.S. military for freeing me from a life of torture; I remember thinking these thoughts through a very large lump in my throat. I also remember thinking these thoughts as I rose up from the ground and stood in awe of the life before me, a life of possibilities. After all, what could be more precious, more desirous or more hopeful than a life filled with possibilities? As I continued walking into my new world I also thought of all that I had survived, about those grim experiences that were behind me. In thinking of the past I became amazed at where I was at and what I was doing, amazed that I was even alive—I was, I decided, a miracle of miracles arrived in Brooklyn, U.S.A., on August 9, 1949. I was a very joyous young man!

12.

I was very happy that day as I stepped off the ship and onto American soil, but also a little nervous, a little apprehensive! I had never met any of my American relatives with whom I was soon to be living. They had all left Europe years before the war had started, so I had never met my father's brother, my father's sister, Bluma, or any of their families in person. Aunt Bluma seemed loving and receptive in her letters! And I was very aware that it was because of her efforts that I was allowed into the country, so I was appreciative of her. Very appreciative...but nevertheless, I was also a stranger in a strange land and I am sure this gave me at least some feelings of insecurity. However, I had very little time to think about it. I would soon enough learn that the younger couple greeting me was my cousin Betty and her husband Irving. Betty and Irving had an automobile and so Aunt Bluma had asked them to pick me up at Boston Harbor.

I was pleasantly surprised. All my apprehensions disappeared as soon as I met Betty and her husband Irving. Both, but especially Betty, were warm, loving and above all, welcoming. They made me feel as if I had known them for a long time even before we reached the car to drive me to Aunt Bluma's. Aunt Bluma was Betty's mother!

It is a little strange, I suppose, but I do not recall what kind of car they had or even what I saw on the drive away from the Harbor. I was so filled with excitement because I was in the United States that I was, at that time, *in a world all of my own*. I must have been very happy for the first time in such a very long time. I know that my heart was pounding with enthusiasm.

Aunt Bluma was warm and very welcoming, too, and her home radiated with the kind of warmth that manifests from the human heart.

As an aside, *I find it most interesting that one can often tell

---

*Perhaps you remember the farm house where I stayed for a few days with the two women who helped me after I crossed the river to enter Czechoslovakia. Their house was filled with love and caring too; an environment that manifested the warmth and kindness of the ladies living there!

how happy or unhappy, how loving or unloving people are by simply entering their home; a house or apartment seems to personify the personality of its inhabitants. Aunt Bluma's house was certainly an extension of her and her husband's kind and caring natures. This was not so true for my Uncle Isidore and his wife, who lived in the same building as Aunt Bluma. They were both polite but, at the same time, cold and aloof.

I first thought that perhaps Uncle Isidore was only distant because he had the temperament of an artist, that he would eventually cozy up as a caring relative, but this never really happened. In fact, I would learn that my brother Moniek had once written him asking him to help him come to America, as Aunt Bluma had helped me. He never even responded to the letter. I think perhaps that I was hurt by him somehow—perhaps I wanted to see my own father's personality in his personality but if this was so, I never did. I also never learned why he and his wife were so cynical but of course, I never inquired. In any case, by the time that I arrived all Aunt Bluma's children were grown and were out on their own, so there was room for me. I was thankful for this, because I did not feel like a burden. In fact, Aunt Bluma and Uncle Morris seemed to enjoy having me as a guest at their kitchen table. I imagine that they missed having children about the house since a house can feel empty when one's children move away.

What I mostly enjoyed was Aunt Bluma's pot roast and vegetable soup and I looked forward to it whenever she cooked it. And, she was the typical mother type, never neglecting to urge me to eat my fill. While, by then, she knew some of my history, she could not know what value food had to me. After all, I had virtually lived in hunger for a half a decade. It is difficult to explain but, yes, even having a plentiful pot roast to eat symbolized my new freedom. I would sometimes have flashes (mental images), however, of the half-cup of horsemeat soup that so often had been my daily rations during my enslavement. I tried not to think about such things, though, because the last thing I ever wanted to do was live in the horrifying past!

My cousin Betty, who always had a smile for me, was a school teacher and as soon as I was rested from the voyage and was settled in my new environment, she was telling me that I should go to school and learn English. I agreed since, of all the languages that I knew, I did not know English and I wanted to learn. Well, the United States was my new home, and so knowing English was essential! I enrolled at Jefferson High School at Betty's suggestion and went there in the evenings. Aunt Bluma and Uncle Morris took care of my expenses!

I remember taking the bus to Jefferson High—the bus ride cost a nickel back then. I also remember Danny, who was the first person I had really gotten to know outside my family. Danny was also a student at Jefferson but I don't recall why he was attending. In any case, we quickly became friends and liked each other very much. Danny was quite the young man, with lots of charm and lots of sincere friendliness. He knew lots of girls and so we began having lots of fun times together. The girls he knew were non-Jewish, but this didn't matter to them or to me. Indeed, I am very pleased to report that I never experienced any anti-Semitism, and so this was the first time in my life I felt that I was free to just be me...and to earn the favor or displeasure of others based on my own merit. This is a feeling that most people feel naturally but, for me, this was a brand new experience. Is it any wonder that I felt such *love and admiration for the United States?

---

*I do not want to sound patronizing or Pollyannaish so I will say here that no, at my age, I am not naïve. I fully realize that there are people in our country who have deeply seated prejudices such as sexism and racism. After all, there is no place on the planet where such ignorance of hateful bias does not exist. Yet, I will also say that such hateful bias in the U.S. is ordinarily in much smaller social pockets than in many other places. But even so, if you have never been the object of brutal and callous hatred because of your race or religion you cannot comprehend those differences in the American culture and those other cultures of the world in which I survived in. And, I will add, that one of the major differences is that the American culture is based on *freedom for all*. Yes, I am also well aware that this country is imperfect in its ideals but, nevertheless, those ideals remain most important to the entire world. And because I was treated with such acceptance when I was a "new American," I remain appreciative to this very day. But of course I am so very well aware that to really understand what I am attempting to explain, you would have to lose your own freedom and be enslaved by a vicious, conquering army as I was, and you would have had to be raised in the Poland that I was raised in!

My friend Danny and I began the greatest of times. As for me, those "great times" we were having were never even imagined. We were going to dances, to the movies and being invited to girl's houses. I had adjusted easily to the "big city" and felt at home there. Even our neighborhood was a mixture of Jews and non-Jews but again, I felt no anti-Semitism, no hatred from anyone. Indeed, people, in general, were friendly and open. Even the parents of the girls I was dating welcomed me and treated me just as they would treat any other young man. I was happy and at peace in this new world of mine. The truth was that I never suspected that such a world existed...I had only hoped that such a world did!

I had picked up English fairly easily. It would be a while before I lost my accent, though. Nevertheless, enter my cousin Betty again. She suggested that I go to Brooklyn Tech High School to learn a trade. After all, I would soon enough have to support myself and begin building a future. I appreciated Betty's help and advice and, in fact, we had become very close as cousins and friends; it felt good to be close to relatives again and Betty, beyond all else, was just a loving and giving human being. Anyway, I decided to become a Dental Technician. This was not a calling of any sort but it sounded like work that would produce a decent wage, so this was probably more of a *"why not"* kind of decision than anything else. I imagine that both Betty and Aunt Bluma might have encouraged my decision, too, although I do not recall this. I know that Irving, Betty's husband, would not have imposed his ideas on me and as far as Morris, Aunt Bluma's husband, he was a quiet, unassuming man and so if deciding to become a Dental Technician wasn't fully my own choice, it would have been the women who helped me make up my mind.

During this time I had kept in touch with my brothers Abe and Seweryn by mail. Seweryn was in Poland but moved to Sweden with his friends and later they all went to Israel together. Abe was in Germany but was able to come to the United States around a year after I did. He had found a sponsor by the name of Katzinger who gave him a job in his department store soon after he arrived and settled in. Abe, incidentally, and his lovely wife, Sala, moved in with Sala's sister Erna, who lived in

Indiana. I was relieved of a lot of worry and concern knowing that at least my two brothers were safe and sound, but I admittedly held some sour feelings for my father's brother Isidore, who had not even responded to Monieck after Monieck had written him for help. While I never said anything, I often thought that it was Isidore's wife, Helen's influence on Isidore, as she was ever as cold in temperament as he was. In this regard, it is also true that Helen often had a *rule-the-roost* attitude and so who knows why Isidore had disregarded Monieck in such a hard-hearted way. On the other hand, had Isidore and his wife shown only a little kindness, Monieck (Moses) and his young bride would have probably been in the U.S. building a life for themselves instead of being murdered by the Nazis and ending up in a Lithuanian grave.

I will digress here a little with the above in mind in order to talk about survival and generosity. I remind you that at my age, I have become a man who has ended up being somewhat of a philosopher, so please be patient. With this in mind, I will share my thoughts on generosity: Over my long years I have heard many men (of all kinds of races and backgrounds) who have bragged about their accomplishments and/or the wealth they have accumulated from their successes. Many of these men have little charity in their hearts, as they are convinced that all others need to rise above their poor circumstances on their own and without assistance from anyone. In fact, they will tell you that they are *"self-made"* and among those that came up in the world without help from anyone. They are very proud individuals, but that pride is built on all kinds of self-deceptions. I say this because there is not one self-made man in the world—*not one*—and there never has been! Everyone has had help from someone as this too is the way that human beings survive. For only one thing Martin Buber says [it is] "through the thou that a person becomes I." (Think about it.) And I say that part of the community of our entire species is based on our generosity toward one another and anyway, that which we give freely and with an open heart is always returned tenfold. I do not think my Uncle Isidore knew this or, if he did, believed this since he was such a cynical man. Nevertheless, I am left to agree with Mahatma Gandhi who told us that *an act of kindness is better than a thousand heads bowed in prayer.* We will talk

93

more about this later in terms of kindness to others being a tool of survival for ourselves.

I was fortunate, as I continued getting lots of help. It wasn't only the financial assistance that kept   me in school; it was encouragement, too. Betty, for example, spent a lot of her time helping me learn English—which I did fairly fast—and during that time we became far more like brother and sister than cousins. I loved her very much and she loved me. Aunt Bluma was very good to me, also, but she could also be very controlling in her way...even with Morris, her husband, who was basically a quiet, passive man. Do not take me wrong; I deeply appreciated all that was being done for me and (as I will never forget) it was Aunt Bluma who sponsored me, but the truth remains that the home was pretty much a matriarchy. Because of this, I began secretly to feel a little "smothered." That is, Aunt Bluma was forever asking me about the details of what I was doing and if I went out on a date, she would not go to bed until I got home. In addition to this she was always at the ready to tell me what she approved of and what she didn't and so it finally reached a point where I began playing a tug-of-war with myself. That is, I reached the point of wanting to move out, but on the other hand, I did not want to hurt Aunt Bluma. And because I did not want to hurt her, I could not tell her that she was making me feel somewhat like a prisoner again and how much I loathed the feeling of having my every move monitored.

Over my many years I have known people who desire to possess all those who they care about and so they put *conditions* on virtually everything the other does. This rises out of the fear of being rejected, I believe, although it is nearly always represented in the guise of deep caring and of unwavering love. In any case, Aunt Bluma's *"smothery"* love only succeeded in sending me away.

Moving out was a very difficult decision for me to make, but it was something I felt I had to do and, the truth is, it was time for me to "stretch my wings" and test my mettle as a young man (in America) on his own. And anyway, I had been a guest at Aunt Bluma's for two years and I also thought that this was long enough to impose on her and

Morris, although neither of them ever made me feel unwelcome or uncared for.

I was also excited and enthusiastic for myself when I moved. After all, one of the most essential lessons a man must learn when he wants to be free is to survive on his own. For me, freedom was the ultimate joy and the grandest treasure to have but I was also aware that it could be misused, and I was determined not to fall into that trap. In fact, at that juncture I was ready to start growing my own life, although I remained uncertain of just how I would begin.

I found my first apartment on Saratoga Avenue in a busy neighborhood made up of both apartment houses and businesses. The small apartment I took was a *walk-up* on the fifth floor. (There was no elevator.) I was destined to eat most of my meals at the cafeteria on the corner because the apartment didn't have a kitchen, and yet the rent was high enough—$35.00 a month.

I was fortunate. My next-door neighbors were Sid and Sylvia Littner, and Sid helped me get a job at a plastic factory where I worked at night. While I managed to also go to school at the time, I ended up not graduating from tech school. Nevertheless, I managed to get a job at a dental laboratory near Times Square in Manhattan, making false teeth and helping in other areas of the lab. I didn't care for the work, but I liked it much better than the plastic factory, where the constant stink of the glue actually made me sick. While I was at the dental laboratory I ate at a cafeteria where they always piled my plate with extra food. I do not know why they took a liking to me but as I think back on it, maybe they saw the tattoo on my arm. If they did, nothing was ever said about it.

I eventually got a job at Gimbels Department Store. I started out working on stock in the basement but after awhile I was transferred to the main floor, where I sold men's apparel. By then I was also working on the 11th floor in the Accounts Payable Department. I didn't like the work there nor did I dislike it but, as far as I was concerned, it was better than either the plastic factory or the dental lab. During all this time I stayed in contact with Aunt Bluma and other family members, and Danny and I remained close friends. We continued to date young ladies and have fun together when we could. In regard to all this, I think I was rather "floating" in my life during this early time of being on my own. For one thing, even though a few years had passed since the war had ended, memories sometimes swept through my mind like little explosions, reminders of those terrible times. When this happened I was always left a little sad, thinking about my parents and others who had perished, and a lot grateful for the opportunity of having my own life in America. I say "a little sad" from the memories of those I loved and who had been murdered, because I learned how to cast those tragic memories out of my head. I had to, or I would have lived in a constant state of depression. After all, one can be enslaved by his past, because when a person lives in his memories he becomes a prisoner of his own mind.

In any case, even after being settled in as I was by then, I never lost gratitude or awareness of the freedoms I had in the United States. And yes, by that time I was aware that there existed some anti-Semitism, even in this land, but the major difference was that in the U.S. it is possible to walk around such obstacles, while other places it is not. And so, *if some people hated you, it became their problem and not yours.* This too is part of the freedom I so loved and respected about my new country. A thought I believe is worth thinking about!

Anyway, while I was working at Gimbels I heard of a job opening in *Sharon Springs. It was at the Sharon Hotel and so I applied. (My boss at Gimbels had given me leave for the summer). I started as a busboy and was given a place to sleep as well as a salary. I slept in a room with other employees that first season but the next summer I was made a waiter and given my own room to sleep in at the hotel.

*Sharon Springs was and remains a small resort village in Schoharie County, New York, and is located in the northwest corner of the town Sharon which, if you know the area, is only around an hour's drive (50 miles) from the capital, Albany. When I went to work there it was an extremely popular place where people came to enjoy the hotels, restaurants and nearby tourist attractions. For example Howe Caverns is a short drive away and the famous Erie Canal is only around ten miles from Sharon Springs but the "Springs" themselves are the major attractions, with the most famous being Gardner Springs. When I was there starting in 1950, the place was having somewhat of a heyday and so tips were plentiful, and this is why I was able to save so much.

The work was hard and there were no days off—I waited tables for breakfast, lunch and dinner seven days a week and afterwards I had to clean the big, red, shiny floor and mop it. The good news is that customers of the hotel began to notice my hard, diligent work and soon enough I was making very good tips. Very good!

I am compelled to digress a little from my story again because I want to share something of extreme importance with you: Under normal living conditions, as I was enjoying in America, the challenges to survive, at least for most people, include earning enough not only to sustain one's lifestyle but to grow one's life and so make their lifestyle better and more secure. This was my challenge, too. After all, I had had everything of value taken from me and so I started out penniless after the war. In addition to this, I also lost the education that would have been mine had the war never come along, and so I was impoverished in this way, too. As you know, the lack of good education is also an impoverishment of a kind.

So what am I getting at?

I am saying that the good news is that no one has to "drown" in their poverty or be "buried" in their despondency. This, to me, is both the magic and majesty of living in a free land: A person can succeed or fail on his or her own volition. And while this might sometimes include a rags to riches story, I am not talking about obtaining great wealth; I am merely talking about, well, surviving in such a way that you have financial comfort and peace of mind. If great wealth follows, all the better, of course, but also know that comfort and peace of mind is of much value, too, since the old axiom is absolutely true—*a lot of money does not deliver happiness.*

With the above in mind, I will tell you that there is a secret to getting ahead and surviving in the free world, and I will share it with you. After all, being free is having the right not only to succeed but, as I have already said...to fail, also. The "secret" that I am speaking of is really not a secret at all, since I believe everyone knows this at heart: No matter what your job—if you are a busboy or stock boy as I have been or if you are an executive in some big business—no matter what you do, *be conscientious in your work* and *put sincerity and caring in your service*. Yes, only these two activities of your freedom will always, always be rewarded. Just always do a little bit extra work and always be helpful to others. That is, give conscientious and caring service to your customers. Even doctors have "customers," you know. They call them patients but they are customers, nevertheless. And by the way, if you run into people who you find are difficult to be nice to, just remember what the philosopher Plato said: *"Be kind because everyone you meet is fighting a hard battle."*

I do not want to sound self-serving here, but I will tell you that anyone who has been a prisoner as I was will know how powerful a kind word or kind touch really is. I will leave you with that thought and return more directly to my story.

The waiter job at the Sharon Hotel was hard work and long hours, but I always did my best to give good and prompt service, to treat everyone special and with respect. I treated customers as my guests, and I was always at the ready to do a little extra for them. In this regard, as you probably know, waiters and waitresses make very little salary and so they must depend on tips. At the end of only my third summer working at The Sharon, I had saved $5,000.00. Five thousand dollars did not make me rich, of course, but in 1953 that was, as is said, quite a nest egg. I didn't know it then, but I would soon enough need it!

98

13.

By 1953 I was feeling good about myself. I had proven that I could survive on my own, I had made friends and yes, I had a nice sum of money tucked away in my sock and so I also had independence. And I had family, too, of course. I tried not to neglect seeing Aunt Bluma and my other relatives from time to time, and so my life was both confident and content. Well, no young man is absolutely content because he has unfulfilled dreams and goals but all in all, I was in good spirits and enjoying life. I must say, however, that even at that juncture I never lost my appreciation for just being alive. And indeed, I would every now and then simply enjoy remembering that the air I was breathing was free. I did not talk about such things to others, but the memories of the death camps never totally disappear and they sometimes return at the oddest times to *haunt* you, no matter how hard you try to leave such memories by the wayside.

Danny and I had remained close friends and, as I said, we continued to double-date and have fun together when time permitted. He also had a friend by the name of Irving, who I had never met. Irving had met a young lady he found attractive, but he was a few years younger than she and so that relationship had gone nowhere. Danny told me the story one night when we were out together. He said that Irving had given him the girl's phone number, as she was a Jewish girl, and he thought that I would like her. I told Danny sure, I'd call.

I did. I still remember the date. It was December 9, 1953. Being honest about it, I was a little nervous because it isn't easy calling a total stranger, a girl that you have never met. And you have to remember that this was 1953. Dating then was more formal than it is today, and the roles of boys and girls—males and females—were more defined. We were not kids, of course, not even teenagers, but still there was a respect and even a little awe for one another's differences and so calling, as I said, *out of a clear blue sky,* and asking for a date was...well, a little intense.

99

I told her that Irving had given me her phone number and that helped to "break the ice." This resulted in making a date. We were to meet on the 13th, at one in the afternoon. Meeting early in the day was Libby's idea. I didn't know it then, but she wanted to meet early in case she didn't like me. If she didn't like me, she could get rid of me early!

Libby lived with her father, Abe Beacher, and her stepmother Mary. I would learn later that Libby's mother Emma had died in 1948 of a rare blood disease and so Libby had had her sorrow, too. Anyway, it was Libby who, some years after her mother's death, had arranged to have her father and Mary start seeing each other, and eventually they were married. (Abe had known Mary since she was a little girl, as she and Emma were sisters. Mary was Libby's aunt!)

The family lived in a six-family house on the third floor—two families lived on each floor in the building. I had time to settle my nerves as I walked up the steps to meet the young lady I had talked with on the phone, wondering what she would be like in person.

I knocked at their door. After a few moments the door opened and Libby was standing before me. It was a wonderful surprise—she was pretty and looked nice in her dress. There was an openness about her, too, a warmth! I didn't know it then, but she liked me, too. Much later she would tell me that she was attracted to my curly hair (which she called beautiful," by the way) and my dimples. Yes, I was flattered. I still am!

The day I met Libby her Aunt Sophie and Uncle Sam were visiting, and so I met some of her family right away. To my relief, they were nice and welcoming, friendly. In fact, while neither Libby nor I knew it at the time, when we left the house, her Aunt Sophie said, *"That is the man Libby is going to marry."*

100

There was a new movie that had opened in Brooklyn called *Kiss Me, Kate* and so that's where we went on our first date. The stars were Howard Keel and Kathryn Grayson and we both enjoyed it. It was a funny romance—a little wacky comedy, really, so we had a fun time. It is always so nice for a couple to laugh together!

After the movie we went out to dinner and after dinner we took the subway back to her house. On the way I invited her to my cousin's wedding, which was on the following Saturday, and I was pleased when she accepted. One reason I wanted her to be at the wedding is that I wanted her to meet my relatives and my relatives to meet her. I already knew I wanted to marry her. I don't know how I knew so soon, but I did.

I think that people know right away when they are right for each other. I had been dating quite a lot before I met Libby, but no other girl had me feel the way Libby did. And this is what I believe makes so many bad marriages—men and women get anxious to find the right person and so they make up their feelings and believe they are real instead of just waiting until they meet that special one who really fulfills them. But how does a person know? As I think about it now, after more than fifty years of being married and still being in love, I am convinced that *when the woman reflects that which is tender in the man and the man reflects that which is strong in the woman, there is that "spark."* And from this "spark" that I am referring to, love evolves. This, I believe, is a major part of what happens between two people who say that *they are meant for each other...like Libby and me!*

Anyway, after dinner and the subway ride, I walked Libby to the door. I did not attempt to kiss her, so we shook hands and said goodnight.

---

*The movie *Kiss Me, Kate* is based on a stage play and tells the story of two-once married, divorced movie actors who are performing the roles of Petruchio and Katherine in Shakespeare's play *The Taming of the Shrew*. The musical in fact is based on this play. It's a wonderful musical that even has the famous choreographer, Bob Fosse, performing in it; directed by George Sidney and written by Dorothy Kingsley. The movie is not the same as the stage play because the stage play is more risqué and MGM was afraid of the censors of 1953. There would be no problem today but back then, being "naughty" in the movies was a very sensitive issue.

My heart was pounding with loving feelings as I walked away from Libby's door, and I was wondering if her heart was pounding, too. I wanted very much for her to like me. And she did—she liked me enough to go to my cousin's wedding, where I was an usher, on the following Saturday for our second date. I had yet another reason for being there—I wanted my family to meet Libby—I was so proud of her and secretly I knew then that she was the one I wanted to marry. I tried not to let this show, of course. On the other hand, after having a good time that day I mustered the courage to kiss her after taking her home. That kiss meant so much to me, and I wore it many times in my memory as I worked at Gimbels that next week.

We went to a neighborhood movie for our third date, and shortly after that New Year's Eve came around. We went to a Broadway show, "In the Summer House," and then to a party afterwards. (I am not sure how much we really enjoyed the play, as it was surrealistic in its way and not very traditional in its storyline although we liked Judith Anderson's performance very much. But that really didn't matter; when romance is blooming, it is not the *doing together* that is important, it is the *being together* that is important—as long as you are together, you are having a good time. (I want whoever is reading these words to remember what I am saying here because I have something to say about this a little later in this book).

The streets were very crowded after 11 p.m. (the time we left the theater)—crowded and noisy! Well, it was New Year's Eve, after all, and people were having a wonderful time in anticipation of midnight chiming in 1954. Libby and I did not stay around as so many people who had watched the play that night were doing, because we were on our way to Brooklyn and a party at the Kings County Hospital that had been orchestrated by the doctors and nurses there. One of my cousins worked at the hospital and he had invited me (and a date) to attend.

The party was quite impressive. There was a ton of food and plenty to drink; there was a live band that played wonderful music, and so Libby and I danced away 1953 and of course kissed again at the stroke of midnight. The party continued on. Then, around two in the morning, I could no longer restrain my feelings. I asked Libby to marry me.

Libby was more cautious than I was and quickly reminded me that we had known each other for only a short time—three weeks! Yet she did not say *no* and instead promised me that she would think about it. Nevertheless, I felt some rejection, but I was not about to let that show. What I did not know at that time, however, was that as soon as I took Libby home—it must have been around three in the morning—she woke up her father and told him that I had proposed and that she was going to accept. Early the next morning she telephoned her Aunt Frances, whose son was getting married that day, and asked if she could bring me so that I could be introduced to the rest of her family. Her aunt said yes, and so Libby asked me to attend with her. I agreed immediately—I didn't care where we were going, I just wanted to be with her again.

This was a big wedding and most of the guests were relatives on Libby's mother's side. They had arrived from Brooklyn, Manhattan, Queens and the Bronx, and we all had a great time. Indeed, we all danced *"the Congo line"* around the room with everyone so happy. In fact, the entire room ended up singing *"Enjoy yourself, It's Later Than You Think."* What was most wonderful, though, is that Libby's relatives liked me and I liked them. But this was not the best news...the best news was that Libby told me that she would marry me, and then she announced it to her family.

All this gladdened my heart and gave me a joy that I cannot describe. And while I think that I was having too much of a good time to be glancing back at the war years, I carried with me an appreciation of simply being alive because of those years. In this regard, I believe that *being alive* meant more to me on that day than ever before. After all, my world had become brighter than it had ever been. I just kept looking at Libby—to me she was the most beautiful girl in the entire world; there was such a sparkle in her eyes! Well, we were in love.

14.

As an older man who has turned out to be somewhat of a philosopher, I have thought much about being in love and love itself. After all, as I have said, I have lived a love story that has lasted for more than a half century. I am going to attempt to tell you as the rest of this book unfolds what makes love lasting, because so many marriages do not survive. Marriage, after all, has its own challenges. And so, some people who were so much in love at the start have relationships that end in many sad situations. I think one reason for this is that *being "in" love* is so exciting while dating, but the loving begins after marriage. I will give the reader this to think about while I get back to sharing my life's journey. I hope you are finding it of interest.

One day not long after Libby agreed to marry me, we sat talking about the future. A first concern of marriage, after all, is in the couple's tomorrows to come. I told Libby about the money I had saved and she was pleased that we would be starting out with at least some financial security beyond my paycheck from Gimbels, which wasn't that much. With one word leading to another, we decided to use the capital that I had to go into business and not buy an expensive engagement ring. Libby had said we must be practical, and so I agreed. Incidentally, it would be thirty-five years after that when she would ask for an engagement ring, but I will share that story a little later.

Our first plan was to marry in April, but my brother Abe could not get time off from his work and so we changed the date to the thirteenth of June, 1954.

As a short aside, 1954 was a most interesting time. In the U.S. the first Salk polio vaccines were given to children to combat that terrible disease, polio; the words "under God" were added to the Pledge of Allegiance; the fear of the Soviet Union clouded over Americans and there were Shelter Signs on just about all federal buildings such as post offices. Some people had built underground shelters in their back yards; President Eisenhower promised more help to South Vietnam and for those who are interested, the New York Stock Exchange had its best year for twenty years, with 573,374,622 shares traded. The American Dream, in the light and shade of it all, was in most people's view and most people had jobs. In a way it was a year of Norman-Rockwell-idealism. In many ways, 1954 was the *good old days* in the making!

About a week before the wedding, a man who owned a market where Libby's mother had shopped said he also owned an apartment house in Brooklyn. Libby talked with this man and asked if he had an apartment available. My apartment just wasn't big enough for us to move into. As it turned out, there was a three room apartment available on Linden Boulevard and 34th Street in Brooklyn. Libby and I went to look at it.

The apartment was on the second story of the five story building. It was three rooms plus a bath. We could afford it! The problem was that in those days apartments were extremely hard to find, and so we slipped the superintendent a few dollars so he would recommend us. He did and Mr. Kaminski called us a few days later and told us the place was ours.

Our wedding took place at a Rabbi's house in the Bensonhurst section of Brooklyn, a private house. We were married in the living room under a *chupa (also spelled chuppa and sometimes hupah), so the wedding was quite traditional. I broke the glass at the end of the ceremony. Incidentally, my Aunt Bluma and Uncle Morris walked me to the chupa and Libby's father and Aunt Mary walked her. My brother Abe and Libby's sister-in-law were waiting for us under the chupa as

---

*For those who might not know, the chupa is a canopy, held up by four poles, traditionally used in Jewish weddings. It is open on all four sides, first of all, as a symbol of hospitality. The chupa also symbolizes the home which begins without furniture and so reminds us that the essence of a Jewish home is the people and not its possessions. There is something else: the tradition goes back to Abraham, whose tent was open for hospitality. In the Hebrew Bible see Joel 2:16; Psalms 19:5. This makes me think of another observation. It is interesting to me that all three major religions on our little planet—Judaism, Christianity and Islam—all trace their roots back to Abraham. Does this not make one think that there would be more cooperation and so more peace and love among us as a species of thinking, feeling human beings?

105

best man and maid of honor. Fortunately, the wedding did not last too long because the living room was very small and there was not enough seating for everyone. My *Uncle Isidore and Libby's Aunt Eve had to stand during the entire ceremony.

We went to Niagara Falls for our honeymoon, but first we stopped in Buffalo, where Sala's sister Erna lived with her family and where my brother Abe and Sala were visiting. We had a good time and spent the night there.

During our stay at Niagara Falls we went on "The Maid of Mist." I would dare say that most people who have honeymooned at this beautiful place have done this. The Maid of Mist is a boat that carries around fifty people—each person is given a raincoat and hat because the boat travels beneath the falls, it is both exciting and enchanting...and lots of fun!

Oh yes, on our way to Canada and before the Falls I wanted to go fishing and so we took a motel. The next day we took a canoe out on the lake and I fished. I didn't know it then, but Libby was praying that I didn't catch anything, as she did not like the idea of killing any living creature. Nevertheless, I caught a fish. It didn't matter; the fish I caught was not five inches long and so I had to throw it back. I did not know then how much this pleased my bride.

There is something else I forgot to mention: After Libby and I knew we were going to marry, she wanted me to learn how to drive. I had not driven before then and she had a 1950 Chevrolet convertible. (1950 was the first year that cars had been built with automatic transmissions). I went to driving school and Libby helped me practice, too, so I passed my driver's license exam the first time. And so I was

*I feel compelled to say that when it comes to my Uncle Isidore, I am in full view that my brother Moniek (Moses) would, with little doubt, still be alive and having a life in America had Uncle Isidore responded to his call for help and someone to sponsor him. And while I fully realize that he was not a warm man; in fact quite cold, I also realize that he was an uneducated man and perhaps to sponsor my brother was too much of a challenge for him; perhaps he feared authority or the complexity of paper work? I do not know and I will never know, but as a fair man, I try to see his side...I try to understand.

driving on our way to Canada, as we wanted to see Niagara Falls from the Canadian side. On our way I accidentally went through a traffic light; it was a three-way light and I didn't realize this. We were signaled over by an officer who had five or six other cars pulled over. When he got to our car he asked for my driver's license and wanted to know if I realized that I had gone through the light and I said, "No, I guess I was distracted, as we are on our honeymoon."

The officer glanced at Libby and said, "You're on your honeymoon?" Libby told him that we were. He gave a kind of grin and handed me back my license, saying, "I wish I was on mine," and told us we could go.

In Canada we went to a restaurant for breakfast where they only spoke French. Thankfully, Libby remembered enough of her high school French to converse with the waitress and order for us. Where we were, however, we did not find the Canadians very friendly. I think that they actually disliked tourists, although the tourist trade was/is their major economic commodity. Whatever it was, neither Libby nor I felt very welcomed but, on the other hand, we both agreed that (from both sides) Niagara Falls was both beautiful and majestic and that we were having a wonderful time.

We had to leave after just one week though. For one thing, Libby wanted to stop in Massachusetts to visit with a girlfriend she hadn't seen for some time; we also wanted to buy some needed things for the new apartment and also, we were obliged to go to a wedding of one of Libby's friends. We had all that to do and Gimbels had only given me two weeks for the honeymoon, so we drove back across the border and started our drive back to Brooklyn.

It is a wonderful thing to be in love and to be with the person you are in love with. I remember having feelings of romance and excitement during the drive home, little flashes of celebration in my mind's eye because the lovely young woman next to me was also my wife. My wife...I was no longer alone...I had a wife! The thought made me happy; Libby made me happy. My only melancholy was that I wished my dear parents could have been there to see how happy I was; to see what a wonderful person I had married; to see how fortunate that I had been. When thoughts like these entered my mind, I became very angry, thinking of the war years and all the unnecessary pain and suffering the Nazis had caused. I did not permit that anger to show! I did not want anyone, especially not my Libby, to know how much inner rage I kept caged in the deepest corridors of my psyche. And so I pushed that part of the past out of my head and thought about how the war had ended and how positive the world was turning again; I glanced over at Libby sitting next to me, and the love I felt for her gave me feelings of joy again. Our trip home went very well.

I was not able to hide my inner anguish for very long. Soon after we returned from our honeymoon, my old nightmares returned. For years I was having *bad* and frightening dreams of being a slave to the Nazis; of the horrors of people dying and suffering, and I was among them! As a result I would cry out in my sleep and this crying out would wake Libby. We would sometimes talk about it, but at other times we would just hold each other or Libby would make sure that I had other things to think about. (We were newlyweds, after all.) She was such a wonderful wife...and friend; I so often found refuge in her arms, in the holding of her hand. Many people are unaware of this, but when couples hold hands for a little while their hearts begin beating at the same pace; there is a oneness that happens; it is as if their consciousness weaves together. This is one of the mysteries of love, perhaps?

Those nightmares that recreated those treacherous times of the war thankfully did not affect me when I was awake. I was very apt at burying such thoughts and memories, and so except at night our lives were normal and positive. In fact, we began talking about having children and also dwelling on going into business for ourselves. After all, that goal was the reason that Libby wore only a gold band—we had always planned on taking the money that would have gone for a lovely diamond and investing it in a business of our own.

Both Libby and I were working at the time. I kept my job at Gimbels and Libby worked for an insurance broker. The only disappointment we had was that there was no pregnancy. Libby was quite upset by this. In fact, one day shortly after we were married, she handed me a pair of dolls—a boy and a girl—saying that they represented the beginning of our family. I was more touched by this than I probably revealed, but Libby knew what this meant to me. She told me that she wanted to have six children, and so for three months we tried without success to become pregnant. Finally Libby began thinking there was something wrong with her, and so she went to her doctor, her cousin. To our relief she was told that she was okay, and in the following month we were expecting our first child. (I was wanting a girl because I was raised in a family of five boys; the thought of having a daughter was precious to me). Nine months later, we named our daughter Emily. The delivery had taken 18 hours. Two years and seven months later we were blessed with a son. We named him Mark.

Before Mark's arrival we were still living in our small apartment on Linden Boulevard, but two of our dear friends—Milt and Jeanette Mandel—knew of a two bedroom apartment that was available at 1866 Ocean Avenue in Brooklyn, where Jeanette's sister rented. We loved it—the apartment was on the ground floor of a six story building and seemed quite luxurious to us after being cooped up in our smaller place. A slight problem was that our rent was slightly more than double what we had been paying—$85.00 per month! We thought that we could manage that, and we did. By then I was working as a sales clerk in a bakery and Libby was staying home with the children. During this time little Emily kept telling us that she wanted a sister and so we made that wish come true. We hadn't planned on this, but Sherry's birth was more than welcomed. And this delivery was extremely easy. Libby's doctor had *hypnotized Libby and told her when he touched her forehead that she would have no labor pains, and that is exactly what happened.

*Some people scoff at hypnosis, but I have always thought that we live much out of our unconscious minds in any case. My terrible nightmares were eruptions from that mysterious world within. I guess while I had become apt at pushing those memories out of my mind, my unconscious was overflowing with them and the only way that it could cope was to push them back into my consciousness while I slept. In any case, hypnosis, worked for Libby.

We were very happy in our lives at that juncture, and our lives were very full. During this time Libby's father moved into the apartment next door to us, and so we had family nearby. Sadly, he and Mary had divorced by then.

As another aside, I want to share a very profound "secret" with you. There are so many couples, once in love, who end up with broken homes. And so, you might be asking, what is the "secret" of a happy marriage? The secret, as I say, is quite profound but also very, very simple: *Through good times and bad, you must remember to be nice to each other.* Yes, that's it! Just always remember to be nice to each other. Anyway, in the interim of all this that I have been sharing about our lives, Libby and I finally went into business for ourselves. I will tell you about that next.

15.

Going back before our children were born, things had gone well over the first years of our marriage. While we struggled financially, we managed to survive and even save a little from time to time. Saving, even a little, is vital to marriage because the old adage forever proves true—*pennies make dollars!* We also enjoyed a wonderful social life along our way, too. For one thing, we had kept in touch with our friend when we lived on Linden Blvd. and we got together often. There were a group of us who would have poker and *mahjong games in their homes once a week, and whoever was hosting the games would be the one to choose some restaurant we'd meet at, and we'd always enjoy dinner together before we would go to that person's house to play. It was great fun, and Libby and I always enjoyed those evenings out.

During this time Libby's cousin who was a baker—he had made our wedding cake—told Libby and me about a bakery for sale in Brooklyn. This excited both Libby and me, as we had been waiting for such an opportunity. What made it such an opportunity is that the bakery did not have to do its own baking, but rather the proprietors (which were soon to be Libby and me) bought their merchandise from another baker.

When one goes into business for himself, or when two people do, as Libby and I had done, there are always high hopes, the perfect metaphor for one's inspiration and expectations. During the process of buying the business, Libby and I had many conversations about our future success, and our hearts were beating with those "high hopes"

---

*Mahjong, for those who don't know, is a game that originated in China. Its meaning, at least when the game was first introduced, was *sparrow*. Like poker, Mahjong takes skill and strategy to win, but luck also plays a vital role. Each player draws a new or discarded tile (or card) with the goal of gaining 4 or 5 melds and one pair. When a player discards a meld any other player can bid or call for it. The game can be a little complex for a beginner, but it's an intriguing game and lots of fun. Like poker, it is a gambling game, as well. Incidentally, I was quite a good poker player back when I was playing and that has always pleased me.

that kept us feeling assured that we were going to make a great success of ourselves. For one thing, the bakery was in the center of a Jewish neighborhood, so why would we not be patronized?

The day we took over the operations was thrilling. For one thing, Libby was at last pregnant and for another we were making some money at the business—not enough money, but enough to keep those "high hopes" in full gear. We also made new acquaintances, also called customers. *Oh, if only we had only done this long ago!*

Whoops, what we didn't know is that this neighborhood was populated with devoted and rigorously religious people, fundamentalists of Judaism! Libby and I were religious in that we attended temple almost regularly but these folks were...well, traditionalists. This meant that we *had* to be closed on Fridays (before sundown) and that we *could not* be seen driving about on Saturdays, or our business would have been immediately empty of customers. Truth told, we put on quite a show of being every bit as devout as everyone else in the neighborhood and managed to stay open for a couple of years. In the end we decided to sell; it was all too much for us and anyway, we were not the kind of people to live in deception. The good news was that we had some money back in our pockets, so we began looking around for another business opportunity.

At last we found a new opportunity in a business that was affordable for us. We bought a sweetshop that was near a hospital. Our thinking was positive—people, after all, bought gifts for their loved ones in the hospital, and we were in the right location. Well, we thought that we were. We soon enough discovered that we only did (real) business on Valentine's Day and during the Christmas season. Once again, we only lasted a couple of years, but this time we could not even sell. Indeed, in the end we just closed the doors and took our loss. That loss was all the money that we had in the world, and by then we had a daughter to be concerned about.

I was fortunate. I found work right away, although we did borrow some (interim) money from Libby's father. I paid him back right away, though, thanks to my employment. What happened was that because we had owned a bakery, I was a member of the Bakers Union and still a paying member. After we gave up the sweet shop, I went to the hall and they gave me a job at a bakery, where I would sell merchandise and also help in the back where I learned to bake.

Baking is a hard job and the heat is fierce most of the time. I did not like it, but at the same time I was thankful for the job. While I did not earn a great deal of money, we managed well. This "management" was much thanks to Libby, who was a bookkeeper by profession and so she kept our home books. She has in fact always done this, and so while we did not become multi-millionaires, we did have security and prosperity in our lives.

Most everyone dreams of being rich, especially in the Western world. One reason for this is because in the western world there are always so many people who have more than you do: bigger homes, nicer cars, more leisure time and so forth. Libby and I had our *high hopes*, too, when we went into business for ourselves. And yes, our losses hurt us a great deal because along with our money, some of our dreams went away also. In fact, after the sweet shop disaster, I wished that I had purchased a most beautiful engagement ring for Libby instead of choosing to risk it on our own business. Everyone makes mistakes along their way, however; people do things that they later regret but I tell you, it is important to muster the courage to leave the errors you've made in life by the wayside and simply travel on. And anyway, who knows what might have happened had I not opened the bakery, for example? I would not have belonged to the union and I might not have gotten a job paying enough to support us. There is much wisdom in the simple old saying that tells us *to see the glass half full and to look at the bright side.*

Looking at the bright side was probably easier for me than many others because I had lived so many years without having anything—not even enough food—so having a wife, an apartment and a child who was healthy was riches to me; just being alive and being in the United States was a wealth of human experience. And so while I wished things had turned out differently, I did not wallow in the losses or the disappointments, and Libby stood just as strong and determined at my side.

In regard to the above, I have heard many people over the years complain because they do not have all they desire. When I hear this, I am forever reminded of what the poet Rainer Maria Rilke said:

If your everyday life seems poor to you, do not accuse it; accuse yourself, tell yourself you are not poet enough to summon up its riches, since for the Creator there is no poverty or poor or unimportant place.

Libby and I did not have much during those early years, but we were thankful for what we had. After all, beyond all else we had each other. We had each other and a lovely daughter!

Soon enough Mark was born and then, when Mark was almost three, Sherry was born. Sherry came along in 1960—the beginning of that decade of rage, rampage and rebellion.

As another aside, I will give you a little history: In the year Sherry was born, Jack Kennedy became the Commander and Chief of the U.S., black people were beginning their trek toward equal rights and 400 hundred Green Berets were sent to Vietnam; that war was just around the corner!

In 1961 we finally achieved getting an American in space but were behind the Russians, whose Soviet Cosmonaut, Yuri Gagarin, had already orbited the earth. And speaking of the Russians, this was the year that our president first met the Soviet leader, Premier Khrushchev. This was also the year that the President launched the Peace Corps. On the other hand, the missile race between Russia and the United States was expanding. In fact, there were so many ballistic missiles between the two superpowers that one reporter said, "Armageddon is as near as pressing a button."

People had learned, however, to live with the threat of nuclear war during the entire 1950s. As for me, I knew—from experience—that worrying about such things was fruitless. And anyway, no one (really) believed that human beings would actually be so irrational as to destroy life on earth as we know it. Nevertheless, in the following year—1962— the world (as we know it) came within "a hair" of total disaster. For a very long week the Russians and Americans were butting heads with challenges of having a thermonuclear confrontation, and the entire world was on edge! When the Cuban Crisis ended everyone, including leadership, responded with a sigh of relief. Jack Kennedy had become a national hero but in the following year, he was assassinated in Dallas Texas. (He was only42 years old).

By 1964 tens of thousands of American youth were warming up to hit the streets as Flower Children, first in protest of social hypocrisies and secondly to become *Hippies in protest of the Vietnam War!* This was the year that the Beatles first came to America, by the way, although I had little, even no interest in such things. And by 1965 we were in a full-fledged war (called a Police Action) in Vietnam. On the home front, there had already been some race rioting but the worst was yet to come.

The above brief tour of those early years of the sixties is only meant as a kind of overview of the times. For the most part, the entire 1950s had been peaceful and, at least for the majority, prosperous. The 1960s were filled with challenges! No matter, I probably did not endure the tension and high anxiety of most others because I had already lived through so many horrors and so much human suffering that I was well equipped to say *whatever will be, will be...*I suppose, truth told, I had become a little stoic in my views but I do not believe I was ever cynical.

During all the above I kept working at the bakery. While I was not happy there, the job kept Libby and me, and the children in food, clothing and shelter—those essentials in all of our lives! Then the *unexpected* arrived!

Hopefully the reader will remember Betty, my cousin, the young woman who greeted me when I first arrived in America, the young woman who helped me learn English and made sure I went to school and finally the young woman who was filled with love and enthusiasm. Well, she and her husband, Irving, had gone to Arizona for vacation. While there, my beloved Betty took ill and died. She was barely in her forties! I was somewhat devastated by the news, as I loved her as a sister. This was the first tragedy I had endured since the war and I was deeply saddened, more so than I could or wanted to express.

Aunt Bluma did not make things easier—I suppose she was far more upset than she revealed, but she began saying that Betty's death was Irving's fault; that he did not take her to a doctor soon enough. (I had talked to Irving and was convinced this was not true at all, but there was no convincing Aunt Bluma, and her children supported Aunt Bluma's suspicions). The other problem was that Libby did not like my aunt at all. For one thing, when we visited her, Aunt Bluma would only speak Yiddish, even though I asked her, as a courtesy, to speak English so Libby could understand what we were talking about and not feel left out. She went right on speaking Yiddish—to this day I do not know why. This had always been a problem and a problem so serious that in our first year of marriage, Libby was actually thinking of divorce.

I cannot say what a position this put me in because I could not put aside, much less forget, that it was thanks to my Aunt Bluma that I was in the United States and had the life that I was having. I told Libby this, but without having any impact. Libby was livid and finally refused to visit Aunt Bluma's at all. At that juncture, I became stubborn and refused to visit her father. Oh yes, I forgot to mention one other incident concerning all this—the first time Aunt Bluma was invited to meet Libby's parents at their home, she arrived wearing white gloves and used them to check for dust. Now I can see what overbearing temerity this was, but at the time I always tried to be the peace-maker and so attempted to justify Aunt Bluma's behavior. In any case, all this

116

caused one of the biggest problems during our early years of marriage. Yet, down deep I fully realized that Aunt Bluma was being overly zealous in her attitudes. Perhaps the answer was that Aunt Bluma was jealous of Libby, just as a mother is sometimes jealous of a son's romantic interests. Perhaps you know what I am talking about: *a mother who thinks no one is good enough for her son and therefore does everything, at least on an unconscious level, to break up romances.* Remember that Aunt Bluma got quite "smothery" with me before I moved out. And so, in this regard, there was truly no reason for Aunt Bluma to only speak Yiddish when Libby was in the room. Yet, as I say, that was all she would speak. Was it a way of saying she didn't think Libby was "Jewish" enough for me? If so, that would have been unfair in the least, but I will never know the answer, anyway.

So at this time the world outside was in turmoil and the world at home was in upset. Our marriage was truly in jeopardy! Then one day we managed to have a long talk and we agreed that we were both being childish. We thankfully got through the crisis and things returned to normal.

While one does not have to *survive* a marriage, a marriage must survive if it is to last. During the time Libby and I were at odds, I learned a couple of great lessons: (1) When there are two points of view, both husband and wife want to do all the talking so they can make their points and overrule the other's opinions, thoughts and feelings. What I learned was that one must instead truly *listen;* to be willing to give up the floor, so to speak, and actually hear what the other has to say. And I will add here that simply listening to one another is a real act of love, love in human action! That is, listening and so caring about what the other has to share is essential to a happy marriage. And (2) I learned that the words of Karl Menninger are true. He states that, *"It is part of the function of marriage for the partners to supply to each other that amount of support and encouragement which is necessary to assuage the wounds and frustration encountered in the daily lives of each."*

I admittedly can be a stubborn man. This was especially true when I was younger. Perhaps it is because I spent those years without the power to direct my own life, simply doing everything I was told or to die. I do not know my unconscious reasoning but I do know that on all levels of consciousness Libby meant the world to me and I did not want to lose her love. But after all, the qualities for keeping love in a marital relationship are both tolerance and understanding one for the other. Without tolerance and understanding, even loving marriages sooner or later fall apart. And so, for a marriage to survive, its occupants must overcome the obstacles because every marriage will have its ups, downs and turnarounds. With this in mind, I will tell you the greatest reason why some marriages last and so many others do not. The reason, I suspect, will be most unexpected by most readers because of its simplicity: What is most cohesive for a marriage is in the *sincere wanting it to last, to survive.* Worthy of thinking about, I believe!

Anyway, both Libby and I wanted our marriage to last and this *"wanting it to last"* helped to get us through a lot of trying times. For one thing, we learned not to take the world out on one another; the world, after all, can be very challenging and upsetting from time to time! In any case, during all this time our children were growing up and even our youngest was soon to start school.

16.

Before going forward with my story, I feel that I owe the reader a little explanation of why I have chosen to bridge the horrors of Nazism, covered in part one of this narrative, to the joys of domestic life on these pages, and talk so much about marriage itself.

You must remember that the Nazis and their followers took family life away from me; they murdered my parents and literally hundreds of other relatives, including two of my brothers. Because of this or at least mostly because of this, I have perhaps a greater passion and appreciation for marriage and family ties; for the importance of home life!

While it has never been my practice to wear my emotions on my sleeve, I will risk doing this at least a little here with the desire to bring both sensitivity and sensibility to my motives.

First, I have spent my life having flashes of what the world was like before the war. While those memories have dimmed for me now, after so many years and at my age, I sometimes still yearn to feel my mother's touch or my father's hand upon my shoulder; I reminisce the voices of so many who I loved and the sharing of their talk, their laughter and their feelings. Indeed, I have so many memories that are dear to me...even the crystal winters of Kielce and walking in the snowfall with my parents and brothers—all bundled up—on our way to visit my uncle and others who perished so tragically and unnecessarily during the war.

Those times and many more that I keep tucked away in my mind's eye and in my heart, with all their scents and sounds, were experiences that the arrogant cruelty of Hitler's armies took away from me. And upon taking those I loved away, those armies tortured and murdered them in the most gruesome of ways. And so when I think of such things as the fires in our old coal stoves that once I thought would burn forever, I am forever reminded of the very meaning of family, not only in the personal lives of people ,but in the whole of society.

Today we see countless children being victims of family breakup and marriages gone sour. We see that the moment life becomes difficult for couples, divorce typically becomes the fast-fix answer. Indeed, the American culture that once called the strength of its cornerstone "family unity" has tucked away such notions in the archives of its past. And so, in view of this, I ask you, what do we have—rich or poor—that is more of value than the cohesiveness of our loved ones (our wives, husbands, children, relatives and friends)? I believe it is that cohesiveness that binds entire nations together and can eventually spread peace around our globe.

If by chance you think that I am being too melancholy here or too old-fashioned, I remind you that you have been warned many times throughout this book that I have become somewhat of a philosopher and, anyway, at my age I can say what I want. It is up to the listener if he or she wants to pay attention to my words or not.

I am going to attempt to make all that I've been talking about more coherent at the ending of this book but for now, you know why I am sharing my views on marriage and family life as part of my life's journey. It is all in memory and in honor of those I lost in the wake of man's inhumanity to man...and for the children who always inherit their parents' world.

In light of all this, while I did not know it at the time, during the 1960s when Libby and I were struggling to keep financially stable and grow our lives together, I was destined to return to Germany. And, in this regard, I remembered the old wisdom to *always expect the unexpected!*

17.

It is nearly impossible to summarize the 1960s. Between 1965 and 69 thousands of—virtually countless—youth had taken to the streets protesting the Vietnam War while advocating *love* and *peace* as the final philosophy for creating a better, happier and safer world. The problem with this "healing" formula for love and peace was that the basic ingredients were "pot" and LSD and so this made much of the Hippy's new world view *hallucinogenic.* Nevertheless, all those youngsters did manage to make many social changes which I think were good. For one thing, they were integral in reducing both sexism and racism. The battle for racial equality turned vicious, however, in race riots that eventually caused many deaths and destroyed large parts of cities across the U.S.

In regard to all this, I remember reading that the Watts riots in California had resulted in 34 deaths, many being injured and around 4,000 peopled jailed. In the next year there were riots and racial violence in Atlanta and Chicago, and in 1967 what the newspapers called the worst riot in U.S. history occurred in Detroit. During this time the war in Vietnam kept escalating. During all this time there would be three shocking assassinations, starting with President Kennedy being murdered in Dallas (1963), *Martin Luther King murdered in Memphis (1968) and Robert Kennedy—Jack Kennedy's brother—murdered in Los Angeles a month later (1968).

Like countless Americans who were hard working family people, I remained a bystander in all the rage and social chaos that was going on, along with the *outrageousness* that was occurring along the

*Dr, Martin Luther King was president of the Southern Christian Leadership Conference and headed up the call for *Civil rights.* During his most famous speech which occurred in Aug of 1963, he said, "*I still have a dream. It is a dream chiefly rooted in the American Dream. I have a dream that one day this nation will rise up and live out the true meaning of its creed: We hold that all men are created equal.*" Dr. King was hated by many and loved by many but since I had seen the result of racism (of anti-Semitism) I was deeply touched by the sentiment and wished that such a creed would spread around the globe. After all, the same creed has been taught by Christianity, Taoism, Hinduism, Buddhism and Judaism. The Talmud teaches the creed in this way: *What is harmful to yourself, do not do to your fellow man.*

way. As I look back, it was during these years that the traditional aspects of marriage and family life were being diminished. In 1963 a lady by the name of Betty Friedan, a psychologist, wrote a book titled *The Feminine Mystique* that basically belittled women living the domestic life of housewives. She told women that they were basically victims, living unfulfilled lives, and as a result, many women responded by doing such things as going braless as a symbol of their newfound freedom and entering the workforce in droves. They demanded jobs in labor, in high executive positions and just about all in between. While I didn't realize it at the time, those wonderful values of America's past termed *Mom, Home and Apple Pie* were virtually made obsolete during the 1960s. I wondered what kind of a world my young children were destined to grow up in. I am going to talk more about this later, since through it all I remain convinced that we can achieve a happier, safer, more loving world, a world where *unnecessary* human suffering simply goes away.

There is just too much to cover when it comes to the 60s, but the dynamics of that decade changed life in the United States and, for that matter, impacted the entire world. Yet ironically, for the vast majority (I was among that count), life continued on not only without radical change but without change at all. That is, we who stayed in the ranks of the working class continued working, continued living from one payday to the next, continued raising our children the best we could and continued striving to build a secure future for ourselves.

During those years of social turbulence and turmoil, Libby and I were going to movies with our children, taking them to ice skate in Prospect Park and even found time to take the two oldest fishing on a boat from Sheepshead Bay. Libby never let me keep the fish I caught, so I always gave them to our superintendent, Jasper, who was always most appreciative. Along our way we also took the children to Radio City and to see Broadway shows. We wanted our children to have the best childhood that we could give them; we wanted them to grow up with good memories, knowing that they were *loved and cared about.

By 1969 Libby had gone back to work—part time—to help augment our income. By then all the children were in school and so this permitted us to make that choice. Anyway, one of the best memories of that special year in our lives came about in July. On July 24th and after traveling 283,000 miles, Neil Armstrong planted the American flag on the moon.

The moon landing created awe in the minds of most. After all, space exploration and the uncovering of the mysteries of the universe had suddenly become possible—quite suddenly children did not want to be cowboys anymore; they wanted to be astronauts. I was astonished. After all, I had been raised in Poland at a time and place where automobiles were a rare sight and many still traveled from place to place on horse and wagon. My world was still amazed by flight, and even radio remained a kind of phenomenon for us; our heat came from coal and wood, and so the gas and electric stoves were a marvel of modern invention, and by the time of the moon flight, electric typewriters remained the tool of great advancement, as most people had no comprehension of the computer—and even by the end of the decade, television had retained its magic for the older generation. And so the idea of men actually going to the moon, of walking on the mysterious surface, was mind boggling, inspirational and, I suppose, a little frightening. After all, the space age, by any other name, had been born and had found its place in our reality.

---

*There is something to be said about this. My helpmate in the writing of this work—Jack Marlando—once interviewed the world renowned cancer surgeon, Bernie Siegel. Doctor Siegel—who likes to be called Bernie—said the most profound and inspirational words to him. A question that Jack asked during the interview is what Bernie would do to make the world safer and kinder, to make the world better than it is. And Bernie replied, *I would say that if you want a better world, love the children now and they will take that love into the next generation with them.*

This was to be our children's world—futuristic and technical, fascinating and unimaginable. I do not think most people comprehended the implications of this feat. I know that as most people, Libby and I talked about it—celebrated it and, at the same time, questioned it. *What would come next?*

What came next was to greatly impact our private life and would impact me personally, since I had finally reached a juncture in my life where I was not haunted so much by the war years. Even my nightmares had stopped being as frequent as they had been. Then a letter arrived from the German Council. They had asked me if I would be willing to come to Germany and testify against a Nazi by the name of Volschlager.

Just seeing the name typed on the page of the letter stirred old feelings—and yes, old hatreds—in me. I knew all too well who Volschlager was. In fact, even seeing his name sent waves of fury through my mind and a sudden shock of old pains racing through my body. Volschlager, after all, was one of the Nazi officers who arrived in my hometown of Kielce when the monsters of the so-called Third Reich first defeated Poland.

Volschlager was no ordinary man, even by German standards at the time. He worked directly under the Chief of the Gestapo and was one of the two man team of executioners. He enjoyed the power he held in his hands to destroy human life, to watch Jews and other "non-desirables" fall into the final grip of death—a psychopath, really! The German ideology simply gave him the freedom to torture, maim and kill, and so he openly wore his assumed autocracy in the sneer of his face and in the strut of his walk. We who knew him and lived to tell about it both despised and feared him. After all, it was Volschlager, too, who decided the fate of his captives; he was the one who sent some to work camps and others to death camps. There is something else. He was the one who would have sent my parents off to die. Is it any wonder, then, that seeing his name gave me feelings that ripped through my very being, that so tormented me?

124

In the letter that I received, I was asked to make a visit to the German Council to discuss my going. I was not ready just to say "yes" and commit myself to the ordeal. Libby and I talked much about it. In regard to these talks, I do not think that I shared all my fears with Libby, but I was perhaps even more reluctant to go back to Europe than I let on. The psyche, after all, can be a very delicate instrument, and I did not know how I would hold up emotionally to it all. In the end both Libby and I agreed that being a witness to Volschlager's treacheries was important...necessary...it was something I needed to do...had to do!

I took little Mark with me when I went to the council. They were very polite and gave Mark toys to play with while we talked. I agreed to go, just as my brother Abe had done a full year before, for the same trial. Knowing that Abe had done it reinforced my thoughts that he too could face the hideous past and remain healthy throughout the ordeal.

Libby could not go with me. The children were all in school, and so she had to stay with them. The council had given me a first class ticket on Lufthansa and so I had wonderful food and drinks during the flight. The flight, incidentally, was smooth and the only (real) bumps along my way were in my own head. I had mixed feelings about stepping on German soil again...stepping on German soil and facing that murderer.

After we landed and I was driven to the hotel where I was to be staying, I was surprised that there were no signs of there ever having been a war. I am not sure what I expected to see after so much time had passed but the normality of city life was everywhere. Remnants of Hitler's Germany and the defeat of his so-called thousand year Reich were all displayed in museums scattered throughout the world, but life in Germany had fully returned to normal by 1969 and even the scars of those terrible times during the war had long before disappeared. In any case, when I disembarked the plane I was greeted by two German women from the Red Cross. Very nice and friendly women!

They drove me to a hotel called Park House in Damstat and that is where I would stay during my stay. All my *expenses were paid.

I was to be at the trial the very next day so I had some anxiety, especially as I lay in bed that night. I know I thought about my family back home, as I was feeling the many miles between Libby, the kids and myself. *What a wonderfully normal family we were!* I remembered when we decided to give the children piano lessons. Both Sherry and Mark were enthusiastic but Emily was not. That was okay; as the old saying goes, *you can lead a horse to water but you can't make him drink.* Anyway, Sherry and Mark practiced diligently and in time began playing quite well. Mark, however, decided that he wanted to switch from piano to violin, and that was okay, too. We wanted our children to have nice things; to have good memories of their childhoods and a good foundation for the rest of their lives.

As I lay in bed that night before the trial I did my best to fill my head with good thoughts. I did not want to dwell on the horrors that I would soon enough be recalling again. In fact, if you, the reader of this material, are a person who has problems falling asleep, practice transcendence. What I mean by this is put good and joyful thoughts in your head; place yourself in places where you'd like to be and doing what you would like to do; use your imagination! You will find that you drift off to sleep easier and when you do, you sleep sounder. Try it!

Under the circumstances, I slept well that first night that I was in Germany, but some anxiety returned to me as I dressed to go to the court. Soon enough, the Red Cross ladies picked me up at the hotel and drove me. Once inside I was shown where to sit and so I followed the instructions. Then the moment arrived. I saw them bring Volschlager in; I recognized him immediately and just as immediately, a rash of old memories flashed before my mind's eye,

*In addition to my hotel and food being paid for, I had also been given $1,000 dollars to cover my costs.

memories of that treacherous, cruel devil lording it over the sick and the helpless, murdering at will and sentencing so many people to death. In those early moments, I wished that I had a gun, as I would have given up everything and shot him just for the appeasement of watching him die.

Yes, yes, I am well aware that such thoughts were cruel, even evil, but I could not help myself—there before me stood a man who had been integral in sending not only my parents but so many of my friends and relatives to Treblinka, to suffer and to be...exterminated. There before me was a man who took (obvious) joy in marching human beings into the forest and firing bullets into them or just shooting them on the street at his own whim. There before me was a man who had murdered women and children—even babies—during the takeover of Kielce. I could not shoot him, of course, but I could desire, with all my will, that he would be hanged.

The Judge, Dr. Rausch, was a soft-spoken man with much empathy in his voice. He asked me if I wanted a translator. I told him that I did. By then I spoke much better English than German.

During the eight days of the trial, I often felt like breaking down; the memories that I was confronted with had opened many old wounds and the pain was in some instances barely bearable. I controlled myself, however. I kept the tears from falling and kept the rage from showing. I conducted myself in a proper manner.

Before and after the procedures, I was always escorted by the ladies from the Red Cross, who even invited me to their homes for dinner. I graciously accepted a couple of times, but mostly I ate in restaurants. I also did a little shopping while I was there. I wanted to bring gifts home to my family. I remember a wonderful feeling in my heart when I bought our son Mark a violin. What a surprise that was going to be!

The major thought that kept my mind appeased during the entire ordeal was that at long last there was going to be some justice. If Volschlager was not hanged, he would spend the rest of his life in prison to dwell on his crimes. And during the trial and after the prisoner was taken away, the judge showed me several albums of Nazis and asked me if I recognized any of them. I recognized a few, and the Judge had both their names and their histories.

I remained in Germany for eight days, and by then I was extremely anxious to return home. The flight back was as smooth as the flight over, and again the food on the plane was very good.

During the flight home I felt good about myself and life again. And although the trial was still in progress, I was glad that justice was at long last going to be done; at least one of the mass murderers was going to pay for what he had done.

Sometime later I would learn that Volschlager was only sentenced to five years, a mere slap on the wrist for all the torturing, suffering and killing he had done. I was depressed and angered by this, as this was not justice...this was a ploy of politics.

18.

I was excited as we touched down; anxious to be home again and anxious to be with my lovely family. Libby and her Uncle Charlie met me at the airport. The gladness I was feeling was soon enough diminished, however. Libby gave me the sad news that her father had passed away only a day before my arrival, on November 7, 1969. He was 79 years old.

I did my best to comfort my Libby and the children, too, were enduring their own pain, but there was little I could do because in such circumstances only time heals the grief.

In time we were back to normal. One of the things that we enjoyed was that Mark and Sherry began playing duets together (piano and violin), and they were really quite good. In fact, to this very day we still have a tape of them playing, "Love is Blue," a song that they did very well together.

And speaking of music, Mr. Gordon, who was the children's piano teacher and who also taught violin, used to score how well the kids were performing, from 1 (being terrible) to 10 (being wonderful), each week. At that time Sherry, Mark and Emily all wanted to have a pet dog and so Libby and I told them that if they earned 10s ten times in a row we would get them a *pooch*. They accomplished this goal and so Libby and I were, in a term, "stuck" to stick to our end of the bargain.

I soon enough drove to the Bide-A-Wee Home in Manhattan and looked for a dog to adopt. I found the cutest one month old puppy, and I instantly knew he would be our choice. This puppy was adorable but there was a problem—he grew up to be one big, cantankerous mutt who liked to bite people when he felt displeased. As it turned out, we had to leave a broom by the door in order to leave the house. It was crazy that we would keep him but...*what do you do?* You have children and you have what has become "their" dog. I will make the very, very long story short—we had him for nine whole years. And I will be honest, I was not *that* sad when he crossed over to that big doghouse in the sky. But, guess what? Two months after he had "gone," our house was robbed. One thing I will say about Butch is that he was a wonderful watch dog.

Anyway, after I returned from Germany and after Libby's father's funeral, life slowly returned to normal for us. And while we had our challenges, we also had some wonderful times along our way, going to movies and plays and other recreations such as ice skating. In fact, this brings me back to something I said earlier. I hope you remember: When dating, the important thing is being together...it simply doesn't matter much what people in love do as long as they are together. After marriage, however, the being together loses its dynamic because married people are together virtually all the time. And so what they do together then becomes important. Husbands and wives need to go out and find things to enjoy, but also it is important that wives and husbands have some of their own interests, too, so they have lots to share and talk about. I must add a bit of wisdom here, however. Over my long years and over fifty years of married life, I tell you a major mistake that many married couples make (especially younger couples): They start out their marriage believing that their mates are supposed to make them happy; to fulfill them with whatever they personally feel is lacking in their lives or...even in their souls. This idea can cause lots of problems for married people, because happiness is one's own responsibility and no one can give it to anyone else. Indeed, Dr. Melvyn Kinder and Dr. Connell Cowan teach us this, and I agree with them:

Marriage was never meant to be the antidote to personal difficulties or dissatisfactions. Yet, for the most of us it assumes that position in our lives.

This is something that all married people should think about, because it is perhaps a most important factor to realize if one's marriage is to last, if one's married life is to survive!

Libby and I became good at choosing to be happy within ourselves and appreciating our lives and our children. We were not rich in financial terms but we were "rich" in our togetherness. We had ample food, clothing and shelter; we also had children, and so I ask, are these not precious commodities in private life? I tell you, they are.

Anyway, shortly after the children were in school, Libby returned to work. (I was still working at the bakery). She worked for an insurance broker by the name of Emanuel Stein. He owned the brokerage company and also owned real estate; he was a very successful man. Then, quite suddenly, he died of a heart attack and his wife took over the business. Her name was Raye.

Raye liked Libby, as she was good at her job and her personality was fluid. That is, she did not crumble under deadline stress, nor did she respond irrationally to challenging situations. Because Libby and Raye had established a strong respect and liking between themselves, Libby asked Raye if she might have a job in the office for me. Libby was well aware that I had been unhappy at the bakery for a very long time. Raye said that she would not ordinarily hire both a husband and wife, but because Libby was so "easygoing" she would consider it. She did and she hired me to be responsible for one of her buildings in the Bronx. I collected the rents, paid incoming bills and made sure the building was well maintained. I was extremely thankful to be away from the bakery, and I liked the responsibilities. I had always been a responsible person, anyway, and so this was, as is said, "right down my alley."

Responsible, indeed! One late afternoon after work and after collecting the rents, I boarded the commuter train at Grand Central Station, as always. There were thousands of dollars in the folder that I carried. I had traveled that same route back to Pelham, where we lived, and a number of times and along the way, I drifted off to sleep. I was awakened by the announcement that we were in Pelham, and the announcement had *jarred* me awake. I rushed off the train...I rushed off the train, leaving my folder on the seat.

I did not think about the folder until the train had sped out of sight, and quite suddenly I was exploding with anxiety. Someone would surely pick up the folder, call it a windfall and go merrily on their way. A single question swept through my mind: *Where would I get the kind of money I would need to make up for the loss?*

When one is in such a mess (such a predicament), self anger twists and turns in one's stomach; there is a nausea that will not erupt but grinds away in the deep intestines—*how could I have done such a thing...How could I have not been more protective of the money...How could I have fallen asleep?* And what about Raye...she had trusted me...she had broken her own rule and hired me regardless of Libby also being in her employ. And finally, what about Libby—what would she be thinking of me? I did not want to go home, but where else was there to go?

Libby was, of course, upset when I told her, but she was also practical. I telephoned the lost and found department of Grand Central Station and thankfully, an honest conductor had found the folder and turned it in. I felt like howling in relief. Instead I simply exhaled; I could actually feel the anxiety leave my body. What could I say but, "Whew!"

In the end, Raye gave me two other buildings to be responsible for, one in Brooklyn and the other in White Plains, New York! In view of this adventure, I can tell you that there is more truth than fiction to Shakespeare when he tells us *all's well that ends well.*

Incidentally, it was during the time that I was taking care of the apartment houses that we began renting a very nice, large apartment in Pelham from Raye Stein. And so, at long last, we had a place with three bedrooms! Mark had his own room, the girls had their room and Libby and I had ours. Libby and I loved the place, but it took time for the children to adjust. After all, they had to leave their schools and also their friends when we moved, and that is never easy. Nevertheless, the apartment was beautiful and had the roominess that we needed. It was also quite costly for those times—$500.00 a month! Nevertheless, with Libby and me both working, we could afford it.

This brings us to a certain summit in my life and so in the life of my family. We found ourselves living a comfortable life, and at a time when we had only normal challenges to cope with. We were making a nice living, our children were in their new schools, and we felt settled. It is a wonderful feeling to feel settled, to feel in control of one's destiny as far as that is possible and, if you will, lean back in one's own armchair and relax. I was still enduring my nightmares even then, but they were less frequent. I guess my unconscious was not ready to throw those experiences away; those experiences, after all, were too ghastly even for time to heal. Nevertheless, we were happy and, as I say, content.

As always the unexpected occurred. Raye Stein sold the insurance business to a man by the name of Herman Weinberg; he was called Hank. He was a nice man, but he turned the real estate business over to a management company and so my services were no longer needed. In a way, I returned to my roots. I took a job at National Shoes In Yonkers selling shoes. In the meanwhile, Libby stayed on with the company and worked as personal secretary, bookkeeper and billing clerk. Life continued on!

I want to share something here, as I think it's important. In so many instances people—especially young people—fall in love and see their marriages as a continuum of romance. Marriage is not romantic, however. The relationship that you have with your spouse is about romance; the marriage, on the other hand, is about making life better for each other than it was when you first met. Marriage is about growing your lives together and making your place in the world comfortable and secure so the *relationship* can celebrate its togetherness. Do you see what I am saying?

Anyway, soon enough our children had graduated from Pelham High school. Our Emily took a job in Manhattan, Sherry went to college, wanting to become a teacher, and Mark decided to go to Pace College and become an accountant. This only lasted for six months. For one thing, Mark had too much energy for a steady diet of office work. He changed to automotive school but he already knew about cars and was very mechanical. He ended up going to work at a gas station that was located just down the street from where we lived.

When Mark was 19 he and a friend bought a van, built a bed in it and traveled together cross-country to California. His stay in California was only supposed to be for the summer, but he liked it and decided that is where he wanted to settle. This move that Mark made was going to change the course of our family's lives but we, of course, did not know it at the time.

133

19.

Life continued on its normal path of having its ups and downs and turnarounds but all in all we continued to be a happy and content family. I could hardly believe it when the new year—1980—arrived. Where had the time gone? It had been 35 years since World War II ended and since Hitler had fallen in defeat...It was somewhat astonishing to me that I was still breathing; I had a wife and grown children in an environment where there was always plenty of food on the table and we were living in a lovely apartment. While there are exceptions, I believe that to most Jewish people, family and family life is important—a top priority! This is part of our tradition, yes, but I think it is also in our heritage. The desire for cohesiveness and unity in our homes and in our communities is in our nature. And so, yes, I admit having a special pride in succeeding as a husband and father. This is not to say I never made errors along my way, but only that I believe that I had become the man—the human being—that my parents would have wanted me to become. After all, even after all those years I still lived in my parents' absence. This "absence" was something that the Nazis had given me that was as permanent on my soul as the tattoo was on my arm. Not 35 years (not one hundred years) diminishes the reality of being taken from one's home and enslaved by the very ones that brutally murdered my parents and so many others that I loved and cared about. While one manages to put such thoughts out of his head, they never go away very far so yes, I say again that I found a certain appeasement in that I believed my parents would have approved of my life and how I had lived it. This too was important to me!

As for our own family, Libby and I were surprised and a little saddened to learn that our son, Mark, had decided to stay in California. For one thing, he was making a living pumping gas at a service station, and we wondered about his future. Only a year later our Emily followed him and began working for Panasonic. As all parents know, it is not an easy thing to let go of one's children, no matter what their age, and we had two of ours living across the country from us. We began going to California for our vacations. Mark wanted us to move to the west coast, but Libby said the names of the streets were too difficult to pronounce. Well, we had spent our lives back east; our way of life persisted there and both friends and relatives were there, not to mention our jobs. No, moving out west was not feasible for us, and we told Mark and Emily *that this was something that we could never do.*

The old saying proves true time after time: *never say never...*Mark met and fell in love with a lovely girl by the name of Stacey. She was his neighbor, they made friends and soon enough they were engaged. Soon enough we would be having grandchildren in California and so both Libby and I agreed that was reason enough to change our minds. We would move! Upon reaching that decision, Libby gave six months notice to Hank Weinberg, I gave notice to my employer and Sherry left Mercy College.

One of our major decisions was to buy a new car. We would need a car in California and anyway, we wanted to drive and see as much of the U.S. as we could. You must realize that even though by then I had seen many changes and witnessed many of the country's challenges along my way, I still carried with me a deep love and respect for America, this land that gave me freedom. And anyway, along with my nightmares and those horrid memories of the war years that haunted me, I never lost sight of the day when I was so weak, so near death that I could hardly move and saw the Americans arriving. I will never forget the feeling of being saved by the soldiers who had come to liberate the people and save them from Hitler's army of thugs and murderers. Perhaps it is difficult, even impossible, for many people to grasp this love for a nation that I have, but if those same people ever lived under tyranny, they would know exactly what I am feeling and what I am talking about.

And so, when the time arrived and we had fulfilled our obligations, we shipped our furniture ahead, packed the Oldsmobile with boxes and left New York the day after Sherry's 23rd birthday. Sherry and I would do the driving.

First we went to Amish country in Pennsylvania. We saw the beautiful farmlands there and saw people of that old religious sect who, in some instances, are still using horse and buggy for transportation and still living life as it was centuries ago; they are an agricultural community and a self-reliant people who adhere conscientiously to the values of family life, a God-loving people who are biblical fundamentalists. In this sense one can discover their entire philosophy in Romans:

"And be ye not conformed to this world, but be ye transformed by the renewing of your mind that ye may prove what is that good, and acceptable, and perfect will of God."

As we experienced this part of America, we made our observations in both curiosity and respect. After Pennsylvania we drove to Baltimore, Maryland, to visit my brother Seweryn and his wife Guina. Seweryn had never married during his life but fell in love at age 70 and married at that age. It was sad in that not long after the marriage, his bride took sick and he spent the next ten years taking care of her. Yes, it is strange how life sometimes evolves for us, but as always that old adage *pops* up again: *the only certainty is uncertainty*.

We visited Abe's son, Sid, and his wife Patti in Ohio and then traveled on to Indiana to visit with Abe and Sala. We wanted to say hellos and goodbyes to those we cared about, since moving far away felt so final. I suppose Libby and I had mixed feelings about our decision. That is, we were excited about our new life but, on the other hand, we were a little anxiety-filled about leaving our old lives behind. The truth, however, is that in life one must always follow their heart. The heart, I believe, is much wiser than the brain. Something to ponder, eh!

As for Libby and me, our hearts were with our children and so whatever anxiety or reluctance we were feeling about making such a major move was soon enough replaced by our anticipation and enthusiasm for the future. What is it that "they" say...*every ending is a new beginning!*

One of our most memorable experiences was visiting Colorado Springs and going to the summit of Pikes Peak. That mountain is magnificent and beautiful, and the drive amidst a forest of pines was enchanting, really. We loved it. Libby, however, wore sandals; neither of us had realized that there would be snow on the peak. We had a wonderful day, nevertheless, and added a wonderful memory to our experiences.

Because the western snows had begun to fall, however, we decided to change our route and instead of going over the pass through Grand Junction and through Utah, we would instead continue on through Arizona and Nevada.

Las Vegas was a sudden shock of neon and flashing lights after driving over so many barren and sparsely populated places; we loved it! We loved the shows, the food and yes, we liked the gambling, too—it was all so much fun; so exciting.

Next stop, Eagle Rock, California!

When Mark decided to stay in California, he asked Libby and me for a little financial help, as he and his friend Doug wanted to buy a house together. We helped him and now we would be renting that same house from them. Soon enough, Doug decided that he wanted to sell his share, and so Libby and I bought him out. We then owned the house 50/50 with Mark. Mark and Stacey had by then moved to Burbank.

In 1987 Mark went into business for himself and was very successful at it; we were proud of him, as we were of both our daughters, Emily and Sherry. And of course we had grandchildren to love and to watch blossom and grow.

In 1983 Libby and I began talking a little about our retirement. We decided to give ourselves another ten years. After all, the future looked bright for us and, while we didn't know it at the time, the future was soon to be looking very bright for the entire world as well. I will give a full account of what I am talking about in the next section of this narrative but, as for Libby and me, we did finally retire. The year was 1993. How had those forty years of our togetherness passed so quickly? Like everyone, we had had our sad and glad times, our struggles and our successes, and we had survived...together. Nevertheless, it sometimes seemed like only yesterday that we stood beneath the chupa making our pledges in marriage. We were so much in love then and our love has never ceased to grow—but after all, we had succeeded in remaining two separate human beings who, at the same time, became one with the other. That is, I suggest, the mystery and majesty of a happy marriage: to remain two separate human beings while, at the very same time, being one with the other.

With the war years aside, I have been a very fortunate man.

SUMMARY

The name is fitting—when Libby and our family experienced the clock striking twelve and bringing in the new millennium, we were living in Camarillo, California's *Leisure Village.* "Leisure"—what a wonderful term! For a man my age, leisure means many things: It means I do not have to live by the dictates of an alarm clock; I can rest, or play or work at will; I can do something or nothing by my own volition; I am virtually free. I say virtually because there are always certain obligations in a person's life that have their demands and challenges. Nevertheless, *being at leisure* gives a person a chance to contemplate his world and, if you will, become at least somewhat of a philosopher. As somewhat of a philosopher I am not beyond being surprised or even shocked, however. As I have said a few times over the course of this book, *always expect the unexpected.* For example, there are people—even groups of people—who believe (or claim to believe) that the Holocaust never happened. While this is as absurd as saying that the Twin Towers of New York never existed, it is said and indeed, it was predicted many years ago that it would be said.

I will tell you here and now that I am among the last few survivors of the Holocaust and what I have told you about it in the first part of this book is not only true, but not even the names I have given are fictitious. On the other hand, it does not give you the full scope of human suffering that the German army, with its Gestapo militants and Nazis, inflicted on multi-millions of human beings. In fact, it hardly shares the torture that I personally went through but, after all, many of my most horrifying memories are kept too deep in the vaults of my psyche to be dredged up. For example, on one of my marches ordered by the Nazis, I happened upon a dead cow by the side of the road. I was so starving and so weak that I actually ate part of the raw lung. Do not gag at this, because many people endured such experiences...and worse! But what I desire to share here is a matter of record and so of history. In fact, the Supreme Commander of the Allied forces at the time, General Dwight D. Eisenhower, said (when he came upon the concentration camps and saw the living skeletons called prisoners) that some time in the future there would be those who would say that the

Holocaust never happened. Because of this foresight, he ordered all possible photographs to be taken and, in addition to this, he collected German people and made them walk through those camps and, in some instances, assist in digging graves.

If this book serves no other purpose I want it to serve as testimony to the Holocaust's reality and in beloved memory of all those prisoners who survived and who did not. The Holocaust, after all, should never be put into the archives of human history, but kept in view so that such hellish atrocities will at last end forever.

Remember in the last chapter I mentioned that in the 1980s the world was looking brighter, too. I will explain: Immediately after the ending of World War II, there began a new threat to world peace. It was called *the Cold War between the Soviet Union* and the *United States.* They were called the "Superpowers" at the time. Actually, these two mammoth war machines had always been distrustful of one another, if not bitter political enemies, so it was only having a mutual enemy—the Germans and their supporters—that gave them reason to "work together" and so fight toward the same ends. In any case, soon after the Germans had been defeated, the old fear and hatred one for the other returned. A major cause of this rapid collapse in the relationship between the U.S.S.R. and U.S.A. was President Truman's order to use the atom bomb against Japan. The Russians clearly had no idea at the time that there existed such a weapon of mass destruction. When they heard about Hiroshima, the *arms race* began and the Soviets quickly began building their own nuclear weapons. The result was that soon enough the two super powers were so equipped with nuclear missiles and bombs that the entire planet was virtually (and constantly) at risk of being destroyed, if not directly from the nuclear explosions, then by the fallout, winds and other toxic results that would follow. As mentioned in an earlier chapter, this almost occurred during the *1961 Cuban Crisis.

*How close did the world actually come to having a nuclear war? The esteemed historian Paul Johnson tells us this: "*On 22 October all American missile crews were placed on 'maximum alert.' Some 800 B47s, 550 B52s, and 70 B58s were prepared with bomb-bays closed for immediate take-off from their dispersal positions. Over the Atlantic were ninety B52s carrying multi-megaton bombs. Nuclear warheads were activated on 100 Atlas, 50 titans and 12 Minuteman missiles, and on American carriers, submarines and overseas bases. All commands were in a state of Defcon-2, the highest state of readiness next to war itself.*"

Had such an exchange occurred, around 500,000 people would have probably been immediately destroyed, and no one really knows how much damage would have occurred worldwide. One thing for sure is that the world would not be as it is today had such an exchange had occurred.

It was in the early 1960s the Berlin Wall was constructed, which was yet another signal that Russia was isolating itself and was unwilling to cooperate in world politics—indeed, the relationship between East and West became even more strained at this juncture. What had happened is that Germany's capital city, along with the rest of Germany had been divided between the conquering powers after the war: the United States, Great Britain, France and the Soviet Union! As a result Russia inherited East Berlin. East Berlin, then, was destined to be communist, while West Berlin was destined to unfold as a democracy. Some reports say that well over 50,000 East Berliners were crossing the border daily to work in the higher paying jobs in the west and so a great many East Berliners were defecting.

And so, in the middle of the night, when most Berliners on both sides were soundly sleeping, military trucks and construction workers were making their way toward the border.

Virtually overnight the Berlin wall was constructed—if East Berliners had relative or friends in the west they would not be permitted to see them again. (All telephone wires to the west were cut to block citizens from communicating with the west). As far as East Berliners working in the west that would no longer be tolerated by the officials—and if an East Berliner tried to cross the wall, he or she would be shot.

*The amazing feat of building a wall that stretched for over one hundred miles shocked most of the rest of the world. After all, its very

---

*It should be noted that the Berlin wall transformed over time. The wall began as a barbed wire fence; a few days later a wall of concrete blocks had been constructed. After this a sturdier wall was built, which was topped with barbed wire. And finally, in 1965 a wall supported with steel girders was constructed. The last version was most impressive, however. That was made of 12-foot slabs with a smooth, slick pipe running across the top to keep climbers from getting across. This wall was built to last lifetimes.

existence was clearly a statement of Russia's harsh dictatorship; after all, an entire people had been virtually imprisoned—their own people! And, because of the wall the *Cold War* became more intense. It wasn't only American and Russians who feared that the Superpowers were sooner or later going to be warring against each other with their arsenal of nukes, but the entire world worried. After all, a nuclear war meant devastating global consequences.

Then arrived Ronald Reagan and his administration to the White House! President Reagan began touting a Star Wars space defense program and his show business past grounded the program in massive P.R. and exaggerated potentials. The timing was perfect: by then Russia was in deep economic trouble and simply could not compete. Thankfully, by then Russia had a commonsense leader, a leader who recognized that the Cold War, while not lost militarily, had been lost economically. It was time for cooperation and so began the process of, at long last, ending the Cold War. The process began with the signing of a treaty between Mikhail Gorbachev and Ronald Reagan in 1987. Actually, the negotiations for a positive ending of the Cold War had begun in 1985, when the entire world began sighing in relief....It wasn't until November 11th and 12th of 1989, however, that the Soviets actually began tearing down the Berlin Wall. As a result, over 20,000 East and West Germans gathered, having what might only be called a gigantic party, a celebration which included street music, tears of joy, laughter and much thanksgiving. After all, it had been nearly three decades since the Berliners had been separated by the tyranny of the East.

My own heart had been gladdened by the news, as I had much empathy for those who had suddenly been freed after so many years. Who would know better than I what enslavement does to a person or about the cold-heartedness of tyrannical bureaucracies and armies?

There have been many wars around the world since the ending of what some people refer to as *the big one...W.W.II.* I remember reading someplace that there are around 300 shooting wars and skirmishes around the world...at all times! Some we hear about, many we do not, but wars of all sizes always produce *unnecessary* suffering and death. In this regard the question is why do we humans not learn from history? Why hasn't the Holocaust been the final example of how cruel and corrupt man's inhumanity has been since the very advent of so-called civilization itself?

In regard to the above, I remember well the thrill of being alive and having my family alive when the turning of the world rang in the new millennium. Was it not time for the world to find peace with itself, to start an age of cooperation and yes, the loving of one's neighbor as one's self? Indeed, I will tell you now that even after those six long and terrible years I spent as a slave, I refused to live in hate. Yes, of course, I endured deep-seated angers and many sorrows but I realized that hate, in its final hour, is always self-destructive. In fact, for a half century I never shared my story with my children because I never wanted them to hate. In fact, the person who was my son's best man at his wedding was of German heritage, a wonderful young man doing his utmost to survive in life, just like we all must do, a human being with his own hopes and dreams and ambitions for the future and, as with the rest of us, with his own challenges, too.

When the year 2000 rolled around, I think most people around the world had positive thoughts for their tomorrows to come but then, only a short time later, on September 11, 2001 came the unexpected suicide attack on New York's World Trade Center, the destruction of the Twin Towers by turning commercial jets, carrying innocent passengers, into weapons. None of those aboard the jets survived the crashes, including the 19 hijackers who were terrorists acting in the causes of religious and political ideologies. Nearly 3000 lives were taken that day...unnecessarily.

Here again the "Hitler-scenario" was repeated. That is, the desire to create one dictatorship in the world and to murder all those who are different and who have their own values, customs and beliefs. No one in the world realizes the danger of what this means more than I do. And so, clearly, the world has not learned from its blood-soaked history but instead has taken a gigantic step backward into a time of ignorance and brutality, a time of hate and prejudice!

Perhaps the reader will remember a popular song from the 1960s. Its lyrics said, *What the world needs now is love...sweet love.* As an older man who has turned out to be somewhat of a philosopher, I ask you, what does our world need more than this?

But where would such universal love begin? I will tell you, not in the halls of Congress or in other palaces of leadership around the world. We have witnessed the failures and even the hypocrisies of the United Nations; that modern day Camelot that has become little more—at least in most instances—than a chessboard for power players. Gandhi said that we all—each of us—must live the changes that we desire for the world. This is why I so sincerely and so enthusiastically advocate family and family life. Love in the home extends to love in the community and love in the community extends to love in the nation and love in the nation extends to love in the world.

You will recall that during those six years that I saw so much death and suffering, when the group of little Jewish children was murdered by the Nazis, I responded by losing my faith and by asking;

If there is a God, then why would such a God permit such horrible tragedies to unfold in human experience?

I have contemplated this question for a very long time and have but one possible conclusion—we humans have been given free will and so we can *choose* to be constructive or destructive...to be kind or cruel. Might this be our greatest challenge to survive and so to grow as a species? I do not claim to know the answer, but I do offer the question since the responsibility of creating a world of love or hate is most obviously in our hands. Perhaps—and, again, as I say, I do not claim to know—but perhaps if the evil acts of human beings were controlled by some divine force, then goodness would necessarily become a dictation. We could not be free under those circumstances and so there would be no progression. I wonder!

What I am fully convinced of is that what most people around the world and in all cultures, tribes and communities want most is simply to love and to be loved. While we all have, if you will, different

144

totems, different costumes and different beliefs, the truth remains that all these differences are merely apparent. We are, after all, all the same when we strip away our indoctrinations—indeed, once we are unarmed from our concepts and denuded, we are all transformed back into simple human beings regardless of our sex, race, creed or religion. After all, we all shed tears and laughter in the same way; we all feel the same lump in our throats when we are hurt by those we care about and the same rejoicing when we are made happy by something or someone. We all experience worry and relief from worry in similar ways, just as we all endure buildups and letdowns in our lives. And, as for simpler things, who among us is not made to feel better by a pat on the back or encouraging word; who has never found refuge in the hug of another or been given strength by someone simply taking hold of their hand? And while there are many different languages around the globe, there are no differences in the world when it comes to a friendly smile and a loving, welcoming glow in one's eyes. And so, in the far reaches of this, the answer to the question that asks, *"Who are you"* the answer is, *"I am you, only in different circumstances."* Something to ponder, is it not?

And yet, with all the above in mind, when those neighbors of ours were given their black uniforms, their pistols and rifles, their tall black books and swastika emblems, they stopped being our neighbors and began being Nazis. This was not a new phenomenon, nor is it an old phenomenon, as this has occurred since the dawning of civilization and it is still occurring today. The jets, for example, that were used as weapons in 2001 had been turned into missiles guided by hate and indoctrination, a terrible, poisonous combination that has been used since the most ancient armies gathered to destroy and pillage other cultures. Indeed, hate and indoctrination was the cornerstone of Hitler's goals and, in these times, what is it that drives a person to murder many innocent people because they are infidels to his beliefs? Again, it is that ancient formula of hate and indoctrination.

I am, as some would say, an old man now. Well, after all, I am looking back over a path of nearly 90 years. Yes, and I am still thinking clearly, I am still walking on my own two feet and I am still living life with my Libby. I know, I can hardly believe it myself when I look into the mirror. Indeed, I am forever saying to the image in the looking glass, *How is it that you are still alive?*

During those six years I spent as a slave of the Nazis I never knew from one moment to the next if I was to be murdered. My life was surrounded with constant death and suffering. In fact, I often wonder how I kept my sanity under such conditions as, over time, I witnessed many prisoners who fell into strange realities of their own minds. Insanity, I suspect, is also (or can be) an escape of sorts and so I suppose there were those who found a safe harbor in its grip. Somehow I managed to keep my rational mind intact and, I am glad to report, so did countless others, including my two surviving brothers.

Survival…the brain of all creatures, including our own, is programmed for this positive purpose. Indeed, it can be said that first and foremost, life is about surviving. During the Cuban Crisis that I have already mentioned a couple of times, when the world came within virtual seconds of nuclear ruin, we human beings worried about the survival of our entire planet. For the younger people of today who did not live through those moments on the edge of annihilation, it was a time of lingering in despairing moments, waiting to see what the two Superpowers were going to do. Our fate was clearly in their hands and if such a war did occur, there would be no winners and possibly no survivors.

Today the human species has nuclear bombs and warheads far more powerful and more destructive than there were back in the '50s and '60s. And so, just as we never want to see another Holocaust occur as it did during the 1940s, we never want to see our world on the brink of destruction again, either. Indeed, it is in fact the time for all of us to become tolerant of and loving toward each other. Our planet, after all, is a very tiny place in the universe—while it may seem very large to us because we are very small, we are all kindred belonging to one extended family. I believe that we need to begin deconstructing all our concepts and indoctrinations of "them" and "us." After all, if we are ever to have peace on our planet, it will have to begin with a simple *live and let live* policy among people, so that policy can grow into community life and expand into nations big and small.

With the above in mind I am going to tell you what it is that makes most people so unhappy in their lives. It is probably the most unhappy-maker there is, and it typically belongs to rich and poor alike. And what is this destructive, depressing thing of which I speak? It is judging others by self and self by others. When countries do this people die, people starve and people suffer. In this regard, one would think, I suppose, that I would be toughened to the cruelty in the world, calloused from my own experiences and from what I have seen. I am not. Tears forever well in my eyes and yes, sometimes even stream down my face when I hear of atrocities caused by the hands of tyrants and fanatics. (And no, I am not ashamed or embarrassed to admit that I am deeply touched and saddened when I hear of especially *unnecessary* human suffering. In this regard my maleness, my manhood, is well demonstrated in how I have lived my life, so I am not at all afraid to show that I have both compassion and empathy for others). With this aside, however, I find it appalling that after knowing so much about the massive torture and slaughter of Jews, gypsies and others during Hitler's rule that any group could be formed to repeat his kind of treachery and cruelty. Yet over the years since that devil lived, there have been many others to take his place. Think of the genocide attempt in Bangladesh in the early 1970s; the genocidal terror that occurred in East Timor from around 1975 to1999; the Delhi Massacre, among the worst gendercidal attempts in modern times; the Bosnia-Herzegovina attempt at genocide (and gendercide) between 1992 and 1995. And of course the entire world is aware of the Rwanda genocide that occurred in 1994. The preceding does not list the horrible massacres, raping and theft that also have occurred during these events of inhumanity and hatefulness.

It is clearly the time for human beings to learn from our own history and begin to change our destiny to one of peace and love among ourselves. Simply surviving in the world and in our private lives is challenging enough! For only one thing, there is enough disease to go around; we do not have to add the virus of hate to the list. And, in this regard, we do not need to have cultures that make it heroic to kill

147

innocent and unarmed people because they are different or do not believe the same as they do. Such arrogance should have been left by the wayside in ancient times. At the writing of this text, it is 2010. Yes, already ten years into the new millennium and while we can land spacecraft on Mars, we cannot find peace with our own kind throughout the world.

But what can we do? most people say. *We are not the tyrants of the world. We do not belong to the ranks of demagogues that run it; we do not lead armies...we are just people living the best we can and as long as we can. So what can we do?*

You can, as Gandhi suggested, become the change that you desire for the world. You can open your hearts to others—to your own family, yes, but also to strangers on the street. You can choose to be kind and thoughtful to others. These are easy things to accomplish if you truly desire to accomplish them. In marriage and family life, an important signal of your loving is simply to really listen to those you care about. For example, learn what is important and of value to your spouse so you can build a lasting life together that is harmonious and happy. Love your children: teach them the principles of compassion and caring. Compassion and caring, after all, are components of love...as Bernie Siegel tells us, *"They will take that love into the next generation with them,"* and because of this the world will become a better, kinder and more loving place.

I sometimes speak in front of classrooms and auditoriums filled with children. I want them to know about the Holocaust. I show them my tattoo, the one that would have eventually marked me for certain death. I want them to take some of my memories with them with hope that they will construct a world that no longer breeds hate, but rather grows love.

With all I am saying here at the conclusion of my story, I want to make it clear that I am not being overly melancholy or maudlin when I speak of love in the way that I do. But this is not just some old man's whim, either. When I decided that I would never look at the world with

148

hate but rather with love, it was on the day I left the recovery home a free human being.

For one thing, I knew that hate works like a boomerang: it does not go very far and quickly returns to you, whereas, on the other hand, love can fill the entire universe.

I suppose that If one examines my life after the Holocaust, they will note that I did not become a Donald Trump, a neurosurgeon or great writer, artist or musician. Indeed, I had quite a modest, hardworking life, but that life never stopped being a wonderful life to me. I had family, you see: for all these years I have had my Libby, who has been the love of my life for, as I have said, well over fifty years now. I have had my children and now I have their children, too. What wealth this is...what success! And with this in mind, I repeat what I said a little earlier—*do not judge others by yourself or yourself by others.* Live and let live and hope that your example will become a teacher for the whole world.

AFTERWORD

There are not many of us left now that lived through the Holocaust, and even veterans who fought so bravely against Hitler's Third Reich are thinning to very few numbers. And so it will not be too many years in the future that the Second World War will be placed in the archives of an all-but-forgotten past. School children and historians will read about it as academic observers, movie buffs will now and then drag out their old, classic war films, but the actual pain and despair of it all will be lost to the winds of time. I thought this was as it should be for quite a few years of my life. In fact, until recently I have spent most of my life keeping the stories and experiences to myself. For one thing, I did not want to upset my family with the horrors of it all or put hate into my children's hearts. And, truth be told, it took me many, many years to be able to confront the memories myself, at least in any objective way.

Even as late as 1993, when the Steven Spielberg movie *Schindler's List* came out, my wife and son, Mark, went to see it without me. I did not want to go but also I could not bring myself to go, either. The story is about how the Nazis start a factory in Poland during the war years, using Jews as slave labor. I did not want such ugly memories back in my head; I did not want to unnecessarily struggle against the old terrors or the old pain. It was not just the cruelty that I personally endured that I did not want at the forefront of my memory. I also did not want to begin dwelling again on my parents, my brothers and so many others who I loved and cared about and begin thinking about the horrors they endured before being murdered. This is not unusual! Most survivors of the Holocaust find it difficult, if not impossible, to share their wartime experiences. After all, it takes decades to come to terms with the agony of that past, and so there are those who never do. For years and years I never dreamed that one day I'd be giving my story in a public forum. Today, however, I speak before classrooms and auditoriums filled with children and teachers of children. Today, I am completing this narrative. Well, as I have said, always expect the unexpected!

When I look into the mirror, I am forever seeing the "unexpected." How is it, I wonder, that I am standing there whole, happy and mindful? Indeed, I am forever amazed at the thought of living through those six bitter years of hell! On the other hand, I am sometimes just as amazed thinking about the wonderful years I have had and continue to have living in America. I do not wish to sound Pollyannaish or patronizing, but I have had only two lady loves through all these wonderful years. Ellis Island stands in the shadow of one, a monument that symbolizes freedom and human hope! Oh, I am well aware that she is an imperfect lady, but even in view of this, she remains a shining light for the rest of the world, and her glow has never dimmed in my own heart. And speaking of my heart, I fell in love with my Libby almost immediately after meeting her so many decades ago. And she has remained my best friend and my wife through all our years together, through the ups and downs and turnarounds of living our lives one with the other.

I suppose that some readers of this story of mine will think my obvious support and advocating for marriage and family life is a bit much for the times; this is the ending of the first decade of the new millennium, after all. But you know, over the years more people have asked me how Libby and I remain so happy and in love than have ever asked me how I survived the Nazis. I have attempted to answer the questions about our relationship in the second half of this book.

Perhaps you recall that in one of the preceding chapters I said that the greatest secret of a happy marriage is simply being nice to one another. Well, I say it again. For only one thing when you are nice to each other you do not take the world out on each other, you do not blame each other for your discontentment or frustrations. When you stop blaming each other, you can then begin to fight the problems in your lives instead of each other—do you see what I am saying?

I believe this is also an antidote for many of the problems in the world. Once we understand that all people are the same as ourselves, that their hunger is as painful as our own, their uncertainties as challenging, their tears as salty and their laughter as hearty, we can

151

begin being nice to each other and once this happens, war will simply go away.

It is time that we begin *fighting* the problems on earth instead of each other, and we have many serious challenges to concern us: the environment, disease, hunger and poverty, only to name a few! And anyway, I will tell you now that war and hatefulness are not a mere unfolding of the world condition, but rather the result of the world's *conditioning.* And so, as somewhat of a philosopher, I daresay that we need to deconstruct our concepts of human differences based on cultural ideologies and religions and reconstruct our world views from the foundation of tolerance and understanding.

Since ancient times all the great teachers in the world have given us a most simple solution to living our lives in peace, love and harmony. They have said to treat others as we, ourselves, would be treated. I ask you, is this so difficult?

And so, I have told my story and shared my thoughts. There is just one last thing I have decided to add. It is a copy of a letter I wrote to Libby on our fiftieth anniversary. I wrote it and asked my son Mark to read it for me, as I could not do it; I was far too emotional and I have never been one to wear my emotions on my sleeve. So Mark read it aloud before our friends and relatives on that special day, at our anniversary celebration. Now a few years have passed since then and I want to say the same thing to Libby again; I want to remind her at the ending of my book that she, beyond all else, is, has been and always will be my forever love.

A star was born, and her name was Libby. The magnetic forces of two continents, East and West, brought us together. I traveled thousands of miles to fulfill my dream. We met through mutual friends over 50 years ago. I had a good friend that I met at Thomas Jefferson High School in Brooklyn, New York. His name was Danny; he introduced me to sweet Libby and I started to date her. Six months before we were married, we went to a New Year's Party which was given by doctors. The party was beautiful and so were YOU, with capital letters. I say, to this day, in a kind of humorous way, that I had too much to drink and proposed to you at the party, but that wasn't the case. The attraction that drew me to propose to you was your kindness, sweet manners and your wisdom.

It took six months to plan our wedding date. We were poor but happy. The love that drew us together overpowered everything. I remember that we didn't have a curtain in our bedroom window. We had to use a sheet. We worked many years, faced hard times, freezing weather, but we made it. The love that we shared and the love toward our kids helped us to overcome everything.

Dear Libby, you did so much volunteer work over the years that I can only compare you to Mrs. Eleanor Roosevelt, and to this day you do the same. I have no regrets, only praise. If I had to do it over again, I would do so with no hesitation. You gave me and our kids a beautiful life. You helped me whenever I needed you. You blessed me with the greatest and most precious family.

Although, I don't say these kind words too often, I have your love, support and kindness in my heart. Let's celebrate our 50th anniversary with good wishes that we want and deserve in life. I don't want to set the world on fire; I want to set "a flame in your heart."

Charles' Family - From Left to Right:
Mark, Adam, Lindsey, Stacey, Libby, Breanna,
Charles, Thomas, Emily, Sherry, Dave.

REFERENCES and SUGGESTED READING

Over the years I did my own reading and wish to share the books that influenced me most.

Buscalia, Leo. Love: Fawcett Crest.

Gaylin, Williams, M.D. Rediscovering Love: Penguin Books

Kinder, Dr. Melvy and Cowan, Dr. Connell. Husbands and Wives: Signet

Liebman, Joshua Loth. Peace of Mind: Simon and Schuster.